Apple Cookbook

Discover the Wonders of Cooking with Fruit with Delicious Apple Recipes

By
BookSumo Press

Published by
http://www.booksumo.com

ENJOY THE RECIPES?

KEEP ON COOKING
WITH 6 MORE FREE COOKBOOKS!

Visit our website and simply enter your email address to join the club and receive your 6 cookbooks.

http://booksumo.com/magnet

https://www.instagram.com/booksumopress/

https://www.facebook.com/booksumo/

LEGAL NOTES

Table of Contents

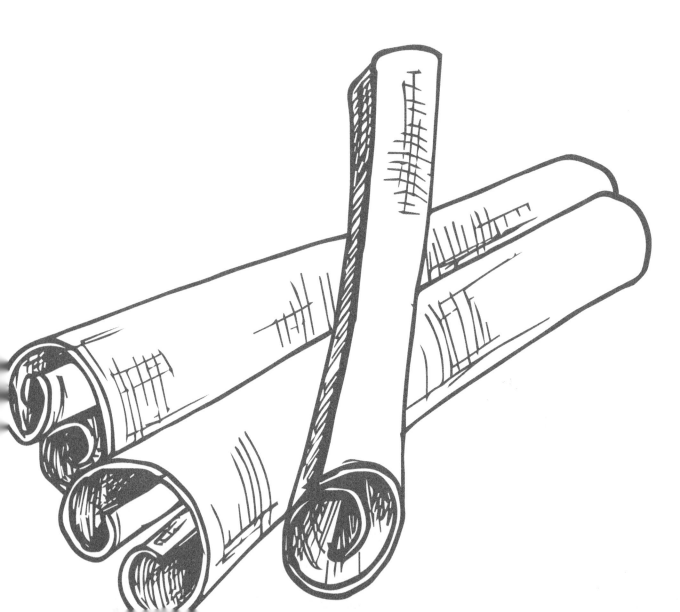

Simply
Divine Apples

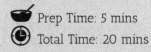 Prep Time: 5 mins

Total Time: 20 mins

Servings per Recipe: 2
Calories	143 kcal
Fat	5.9 g
Carbohydrates	24.3g
Protein	0.4 g
Cholesterol	15 mg
Sodium	45 mg

Ingredients

1/4 C. butter
4 large tart apples - peeled, cored and
sliced 1/4 inch thick
2 tsp cornstarch
1/2 C. cold water

1/2 C. brown sugar
1/2 tsp ground cinnamon

Directions

1. In a large skillet, melt the butter on medium heat and cook the apples for about 6-7 minutes, stirring continuously.
2. In a bowl, mix together the water and cornstarch.
3. Add the cornstarch mixture and stir to combine.
4. Stir in the brown sugar and cinnamon and boil for about 2 minutes, stirring occasionally.
5. Serve warm.

INDESCRIBABLY
Yummy Apple Dumplings

🥣 Prep Time: 20 mins

🕐 Total Time: 1 hr 5 mins

Servings per Recipe: 16

Calories	333 kcal
Fat	19 g
Carbohydrates	38.5g
Protein	2.7 g
Cholesterol	31 mg
Sodium	360 mg

Ingredients

2 large Granny Smith apples, peeled,
cored and cut each apple in 8 wedges
2 (10 oz.) cans refrigerated crescent roll
dough
1 C. butter
1 1/2 C. white sugar

1 tsp ground cinnamon
1 (12 fluid oz.) can Mountain Dew

Directions

1. Set your oven to 350 degrees F before doing anything else and grease a 13x9-inch baking dish.
2. Separate the crescent roll dough into triangles.
3. Place 1 apple wedge over a dough piece and roll the triangle around the apple wedge.
4. With your hands, pinch to seal the roll.
5. Arrange the dumplings onto the prepared baking dish in a single layer.
6. In a small pan, melt the butter and add the cinnamon and sugar and stir to combine.
7. Place the butter mixture over the dumplings evenly and top with the Mountain Dew.
8. Cook everything in the oven for about 35-45 minutes.

Moist
Apple Snack

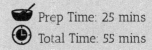 Prep Time: 25 mins

Total Time: 55 mins

Servings per Recipe: 16

Calories	143 kcal
Fat	5.7 g
Carbohydrates	22.1g
Protein	1.8 g
Cholesterol	19 mg
Sodium	94 mg

Ingredients

1 C. sifted all-purpose flour
1 tsp baking powder
1/4 tsp salt
1/4 tsp ground cinnamon
1/4 C. butter, melted
1/2 C. packed brown sugar
1/2 C. white sugar
1 egg

1 tsp vanilla extract
1/2 C. chopped apple
1/2 C. finely chopped walnuts
2 tbsp white sugar
2 tsp ground cinnamon

Directions

1. Set your oven to 350 degrees F before doing anything else and lightly, grease a 9x9-inch baking dish.
2. In a large bowl, sift together the flour, baking powder, 1/4 tsp of cinnamon and salt.
3. In another bowl, add the butter, 1/2 C. of white sugar and brown sugar and mix till smooth.
4. Add the egg and vanilla and stir to combine.
5. Add the egg mixture into the flour mixture and mix till well combined.
6. Fold in the apples and walnuts and transfer the mixture onto the prepared baking dish evenly.
7. In a small bowl, mix together the remaining white sugar and cinnamon and sprinkle over the apple mixture.
8. Cook everything in the oven for about 25-30 minutes.
9. Remove everything from the oven and keep aside to cool completely.
10. Cut everything into equal sized squares and serve.

HEALTHIER
Apple & Oat Crisp

Prep Time: 30 mins
Total Time: 1 hr 20 mins

Servings per Recipe: 12

Calories	316 kcal
Fat	8.4 g
Carbohydrates	60.5g
Protein	2.4 g
Cholesterol	20 mg
Sodium	98 mg

Ingredients

10 C. apples, peeled, cored and sliced
1 C. white sugar
1 tbsp all-purpose flour
1 tsp ground cinnamon
1/2 C. water
1 C. quick-cooking oats

1 C. all-purpose flour
1 C. packed brown sugar
1/4 tsp baking powder
1/4 tsp baking soda
1/2 C. butter, melted

Directions

1. Set your oven to 350 degrees F before doing anything else and lightly, grease a 13x9-inch baking dish.
2. Place the apple slices in the bottom of the prepared baking dish evenly.
3. In a bowl, mix together white sugar, cinnamon and 1 tbsp of the flour and sprinkle over the apple slices evenly.
4. Drizzle the water over the apple slices evenly.
5. In another bowl, add the remaining ingredients and mix till a coarse crumb forms.
6. Spread the crumb mixture over the apple slices evenly and cook everything in the oven for about 45 minutes.

English Teatime Apple Treat

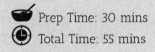

Prep Time: 30 mins
Total Time: 55 mins

Servings per Recipe: 168

Calories	562 kcal
Fat	25.9 g
Carbohydrates	80g
Protein	4.8 g
Cholesterol	8 mg
Sodium	184 mg

Ingredients

2 tbsp lemon juice
4 C. water
4 Granny Smith apples - peeled, cored and sliced
2 tbsp butter
1 C. brown sugar
1 tsp ground cinnamon
1 tbsp cornstarch

1 tbsp water
1 (17.25 oz.) package frozen puff pastry sheets, thawed
1 C. confectioners' sugar
1 tbsp milk
1 tsp vanilla extract

Directions

1. Set your oven to 400 degrees F before doing anything else.
2. In a large bowl, mix together the apple slices, lemon juice and 4 C. of the water and keep aside before using.
3. Drain the apple slices completely.
4. In a large skillet, melt the butter on medium heat and cook the apple slices for about 2 minutes, stirring continuously.
5. Stir in the cinnamon and brown sugar and cook everything for about 2 minutes, stirring continuously.
6. In a bowl, mix together 1 tbsp of the water and cornstarch.
7. Add the cornstarch mixture into the skillet and cook, stirring for about 1 minute.
8. Remove from the heat and keep aside to cool slightly.
9. Unfold the pastry sheets and cut each one into a large square.
10. Cut each large square into 4 small squares.
11. Divide the apple mixture in the center of each square and fold into a triangle shape, by turning from the corner to corner.
12. With your hands, pinch the edges to seal tightly.

13. Arrange the turnovers onto a baking sheet in a single layer about 1-inch apart and cook everything in the oven for about 25 minutes.

14. Remove everything from the oven and keep aside to cool completely.

15. Meanwhile for the glaze in a small bowl, mix together the remaining ingredients.

16. Pour the glaze over the turnovers and serve.

American
Apple Pie

Prep Time: 30 mins
Total Time: 1 hr 15 mins

Servings per Recipe: 8
Calories	278 kcal
Fat	11.8 g
Carbohydrates	43.5g
Protein	1.6 g
Cholesterol	31 mg
Sodium	83 mg

Ingredients

4 C. thinly sliced apples
1/4 C. orange juice
3/4 C. all-purpose flour
1 C. white sugar
1/2 tsp ground cinnamon

1/4 tsp ground nutmeg
1 pinch salt
1/2 C. butter

Directions

1. Set your oven to 375 degrees F before doing anything else and lightly, grease a 9-inch pie dish.
2. Arrange the apple slices in the bottom of the prepared pie dish evenly and drizzle with the orange juice.
3. In a bowl, mix together the remaining ingredients except the butter.
4. With a pastry cutter, cut the butter in the flour mixture and mix till a coarse crumb forms.
5. Place the crumb mixture over the apple slices evenly and cook everything in the oven for about 45 minutes.
6. Serve warm.

CHILDHOOD
Memory Dip for Apple Slices

Prep Time: 5 mins
Total Time: 10 mins

Servings per Recipe: 8
Calories	137 kcal
Fat	9.8 g
Carbohydrates	9.8g
Protein	2.1 g
Cholesterol	31 mg
Sodium	86 mg

Ingredients

1 (8 oz.) package cream cheese
1/2 C. brown sugar
1 tbsp vanilla extract

Directions

1. In a bowl, add all the ingredients and mix till the sugar is dissolved completely and smooth.

New England
Apple Cookies

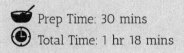 Prep Time: 30 mins

Total Time: 1 hr 18 mins

Servings per Recipe: 60
Calories	77 kcal
Fat	2.8 g
Carbohydrates	12.7g
Protein	0.9 g
Cholesterol	7 mg
Sodium	55 mg

Ingredients

2 C. all-purpose flour
1 tsp baking soda
1 tsp ground cinnamon
1 tsp ground cloves
1/2 tsp ground nutmeg
1/2 tsp salt
1/2 C. softened butter
1 1/2 C. packed brown sugar

1 egg, beaten
1 C. chopped walnuts
1 C. chopped apples
1 C. raisins
2/3 C. confectioners' sugar
1 tbsp milk

Directions

1. Set your oven to 350 degrees F before doing anything else and line the cookie sheets with parchment papers.
2. In a large bowl, sift together the flour, baking soda, spices and salt.
3. In another bowl, add the butter and beat till fluffy and light.
4. Add the egg and sugar and mix till well combined.
5. Add the egg mixture into the flour mixture and mix till well combined.
6. Fold in the apples, raisins and walnuts.
7. With a teaspoon, place the mixture onto the prepared cookie sheets in a single layer about 1 1/2-inches apart.
8. Cook everything in the oven for about 12-14 minutes.
9. Remove everything from the oven and keep aside on wire racks to cool completely.
10. Meanwhile for the glaze in a small bowl, mix together the remaining ingredients.
11. Pour the glaze over the cookies and serve.

APPLE BREAD
in Ogunquit Style

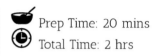 Prep Time: 20 mins

Total Time: 2 hrs

Servings per Recipe: 16	
Calories	377 kcal
Fat	19.6 g
Carbohydrates	47.4g
Protein	4.8 g
Cholesterol	35 mg
Sodium	238 mg

Ingredients

cooking spray
3 C. all-purpose flour
1 tsp baking soda
1 tsp salt
1 C. chopped walnuts
3 C. apples - peeled, cored, and chopped

1 C. vegetable oil
2 C. white sugar
3 eggs, beaten
2 tsp ground cinnamon

Directions

1. Set your oven to 300 degrees F before doing anything else and grease 2 (8 1/2x4 1/2-inch) loaf pans.
2. In a large bowl, mix together the flour, baking soda, cinnamon and salt.
3. In another bowl, add the eggs, sugar and oil and beat till well combined.
4. Add the egg mixture into the flour mixture and mix till well combined.
5. Fold in the apples and walnuts.
6. Transfer the mixture onto the prepared loaf pans evenly. and cook everything in the oven for about 90 minutes or till a toothpick inserted in the center comes out clean.
7. Remove everything from the oven and keep aside for about 10 minutes to cool before removing from the loaf pans.

Mexican Style
Apple Dessert

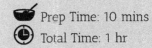 Prep Time: 10 mins

Total Time: 1 hr

Servings per Recipe: 6

Calories	530 kcal
Fat	18.9 g
Carbohydrates	88.2g
Protein	4.6 g
Cholesterol	41 mg
Sodium	392 mg

Ingredients

1 (21 oz.) can apple pie filling
6 (8 inch) flour tortillas
1 tsp ground cinnamon
1/2 C. butter
1/2 C. white sugar

1/2 C. brown sugar
1/2 C. water

Directions

1. Set your oven to 350 degrees F before doing anything else and lightly, grease a large baking dish.
2. Divide the pie filling in the center of each tortilla evenly and sprinkle with the cinnamon.
3. Roll each tortilla, tucking in the edges and arrange them into the prepared baking dish, seam-side down.
4. In a pan, mix together the remaining ingredients on medium heat.
5. Bring everything to a boil, stirring continuously.
6. Reduce the heat and simmer for about 3 minutes.
7. Place the butter mixture over the enchiladas evenly and cook everything in the oven for about 20 minutes.

COMFORTING
Apples

🍲 Prep Time: 5 mins
🕐 Total Time: 20 mins

Servings per Recipe: 8

Calories	110 kcal
Fat	0.2 g
Carbohydrates	28.8g
Protein	0.4 g
Cholesterol	0 mg
Sodium	4 mg

Ingredients

8 Granny Smith apples, peeled, cored,
and sliced
2 tbsp white sugar

1 tsp lemon juice
1/4 C. cinnamon red hot candies

Directions

1. In a large microwave-safe bowl, mix together all the ingredients.
2. Microwave on high for about 15 minutes, stirring every 5 minutes.
3. Serve warm or refrigerate to chill.

Danish
Apple Pastries

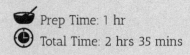 Prep Time: 1 hr

Total Time: 2 hrs 35 mins

Servings per Recipe: 8

Calories	337 kcal
Fat	10.6 g
Carbohydrates	57.7g
Protein	4 g
Cholesterol	27 mg
Sodium	443 mg

Ingredients

Dough:
2 C. all-purpose flour
2 tbsp packed brown sugar
1 tsp salt
1 1/2 tsp instant yeast
3/4 C. hot water
2 tbsp butter at room temperature
Filling:
2 1/2 C. apples - peeled, cored, and chopped
3 tbsp butter
1/2 C. packed brown sugar

1 1/2 tbsp all-purpose flour
1/4 tsp salt
1/4 tsp ground cinnamon
1/4 tsp ground nutmeg
Glaze:
2 tbsp butter
2/3 C. confectioners' sugar
1/2 tsp vanilla extract
4 tsp milk

Directions

1. In a large bowl, mix together 1 C. of the flour, instant yeast, 2 tbsp of the brown sugar and 1 teaspoon of the salt.
2. Add the butter and water and beat till well combined.
3. Add the remaining flour and beat till well combined.
4. Place the dough onto lightly floured surface and with your hands, knead the dough for about 10 minutes.
5. Make a large ball from the dough and place into a greased bowl.
6. Turn the dough ball in the bowl evenly.
7. With plastic wrap, cover the bowl and keep aside for about 1 hour.
8. Meanwhile for the filling, in a bowl, mix together 1 1/2 tbsp of the flour, 1/2 C. of the brown sugar, cinnamon, nutmeg and 1/4 tsp of the salt.
9. In a medium pan, mix together 3 tbsp of the butter, apples and the flour mixture on

medium-high heat.

10. Bring everything to a boil and reduce the heat to low.
11. Simmer for about 5 minutes and remove everything from the heat, then keep aside to cool completely.
12. Now, place the dough onto a floured surface and with your hands, punch it down.
13. Cover and keep everything on a floured surface for about 15 minutes.
14. With a rolling pin, roll the dough into a 13x8-inch rectangle.
15. Arrange the dough rectangle onto a greased baking sheet.
16. Carefully, turn the baking sheet onto a smooth surface.
17. Place the filling mixture over the center third of the dough.
18. With a sharp knife, make the cuts in the dough along the right side, starting each cut about 1/4 inch from the filling mixture.
19. Cut to the edge of the dough strip, with each cut angled to about 4 o'clock.
20. Each strip of dough should be about 1-inch thick.
21. Repeat with the left side of the dough, angling the cuts to 8 o'clock.
22. From the top, fold the dough strips across the filling mixture, alternating left and right.
23. With your hands, pinch the top and bottom ends of the pastry to seal in the filling.
24. With a plastic wrap, cover the pastry and keep it at room temperature for about 30-40 minutes.
25. Set your oven to 375 degrees F.
26. Arrange the pastry on the baking sheet and cook everything in the oven for about 10 minutes.
27. Now, cover everything with a sheet of foil and cook it all in the oven for about 10 minutes more.
28. Remove everything from the oven and keep it aside to cool completely.
29. Meanwhile for the glaze in a pan, heat the butter on medium heat.
30. Cook everything for about 5 minutes, swirling the pan occasionally.
31. Transfer into a bowl and keep aside to cool slightly.
32. Add the vanilla extract and confectioners' sugar and stir to combine.
33. Slowly, add the milk, stirring continuously till well combined.
34. Pour the glaze over the pastry and serve.

Thanksgiving
Apple Stuffing

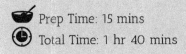 Prep Time: 15 mins

Total Time: 1 hr 40 mins

Servings per Recipe: 10
Calories	235 kcal
Fat	11.6 g
Carbohydrates	21.7g
Protein	12.5 g
Cholesterol	80 mg
Sodium	548 mg

Ingredients

1 1/2 C. cubed whole wheat bread
3 3/4 C. cubed white bread
1 lb. ground turkey sausage
1 C. chopped onion
3/4 C. chopped celery
2 1/2 tsp dried sage
1 1/2 tsp dried rosemary
1/2 tsp dried thyme

1 Golden Delicious apple, cored and chopped
3/4 C. dried cranberries
1/3 C. minced fresh parsley
1 cooked turkey liver, finely chopped
3/4 C. turkey stock
4 tbsp unsalted butter, melted

Directions

1. Set your oven to 350 degrees F before doing anything else.
2. In a large baking sheet, place the bread cubes in a single layer and cook everything in the oven for about 5-7 minutes.
3. Place the toasted bread cubes in a large bowl.
4. Heat a large skillet on medium heat and cook the sausage and onion till browned, breaking up the sausage into small pieces.
5. Stir in the celery and herbs and cook, stirring continuously for about 2 minutes.
6. Add the sausage mixture in the bowl with bread cubes.
7. Add the liver, apple, cranberries and parsley and mix well.
8. Drizzle with the melted butter and broth and gently stir to combine.

KEEPER
Apple Butter

🍲 Prep Time: 30 mins

🕐 Total Time: 11 hrs 30 mins

Servings per Recipe: 128

Calories	34 kcal
Fat	0 g
Carbohydrates	9g
Protein	0.1 g
Cholesterol	0 mg
Sodium	5 mg

Ingredients

5 1/2 lb. apples - peeled, cored and finely chopped
4 C. white sugar
2 tsp ground cinnamon

1/4 tsp ground cloves
1/4 tsp salt

Directions

1. In a slow cooker, place all the ingredients and mix well.
2. Set the slow cooker on High and cook, covered for about 1 hour.
3. Now, set the slow cooker on Low and cook, covered for about 9 - 11 hours.
4. Uncover the slow cooker and cook everything for about 1 hour more.
5. With a hand beater, smooth the butter and transfer into sterilized containers.
6. Cover tightly and preserve in the refrigerator.

Countryside
Apple Pie

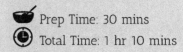 Prep Time: 30 mins
🕐 Total Time: 1 hr 10 mins

Servings per Recipe: 8
Calories	358 kcal
Fat	16.4 g
Carbohydrates	52g
Protein	2.5 g
Cholesterol	23 mg
Sodium	210 mg

Ingredients

1 (9 inch) deep dish pie crust
5 C. apples - peeled, cored and thinly sliced
1/2 C. white sugar
3/4 tsp ground cinnamon
1/3 C. white sugar

3/4 C. all-purpose flour
6 tbsp butter

Directions

1. Set your oven to 400 degrees F before doing anything else.
2. In an unbaked pie shell, place the sliced apples.
3. In a small bowl, mix together 1/2 C. of the sugar and cinnamon and sprinkle over the apple slices.
4. In another bowl, mix together the flour and the remaining sugar.
5. With a pastry cutter, cut the butter and mix till a crumbly mixture forms.
6. Place the mixture over the apple slices evenly and cook everything in the oven for about 40 minutes.

FALL SEASON
Apple Muffins

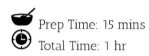

Prep Time: 15 mins
Total Time: 1 hr

Servings per Recipe: 18

Calories	249 kcal
Fat	8 g
Carbohydrates	42.6g
Protein	2.8 g
Cholesterol	23 mg
Sodium	182 mg

Ingredients

2 1/2 C. all-purpose flour
2 C. white sugar
1 tbsp pumpkin pie spice
1 tsp baking soda
1/2 tsp salt
2 eggs, lightly beaten
1 C. canned pumpkin puree
1/2 C. vegetable oil

2 C. peeled, cored and chopped apple
2 tbsp all-purpose flour
1/4 C. white sugar
1/2 tsp ground cinnamon
4 tsp butter

Directions

1. Set your oven to 350 degrees F before doing anything else and lightly, grease 18 cups of muffin trays.
2. In a large bowl, sift together 2 1/2 C. of the flour, baking soda, 2 C. of the sugar, pumpkin pie spice and salt.
3. In another bowl, add the eggs, oil and pumpkin and beat till well combined.
4. Add the egg mixture into the flour mixture and mix till well combined.
5. Fold in the apples and transfer the mixture onto the prepared muffin cups evenly.
6. In another bowl, mix together the remaining flour, sugar and cinnamon.
7. With a pastry cutter, cut the butter and mix till a coarse crumb forms.
8. Place the mixture over each muffin evenly and cook everything in the oven for about 35-40 minutes or till a toothpick inserted in the center comes out clean.

Appealing
Apple Beverage

Prep Time: 10 mins
Total Time: 10 mins

Servings per Recipe: 12
Calories	168 kcal
Fat	0.1 g
Carbohydrates	42.1g
Protein	0.2 g
Cholesterol	0 mg
Sodium	19 mg

Ingredients

1 (32 fluid oz.) bottle apple juice, chilled
1 (12 fluid oz.) can frozen cranberry juice concentrate
1 C. orange juice

1 1/2 liters ginger ale
1 apple

Directions

1. In a large punch bowl, add the apple juice, orange juice and cranberry juice concentrate and stir till dissolved completely.
2. Slowly, pour the ginger ale on top.
3. Cut the apple thinly in vertical slices.
4. Place the apple slices on the top in the punch bowl.

EASIEST
Apple Crisp

Prep Time: 20 mins
Total Time: 1 hr

Servings per Recipe: 6

Calories	361 kcal
Fat	15.6 g
Carbohydrates	55.7g
Protein	2 g
Cholesterol	41 mg
Sodium	110 mg

Ingredients

4 C. apples - peeled, cored, and sliced
1 tsp ground cinnamon
1 C. white sugar
3/4 C. all-purpose flour

1/2 C. cold butter

Directions

1. Set your oven to 350 degrees F before doing anything else and lightly, grease an 8x8-inch casserole dish.
2. Place the apple slices in the bottom of the prepared baking dish evenly.
3. Sprinkle with the cinnamon and drizzle with the water evenly.
4. In a bowl, mix together the sugar and flour.
5. With a pastry cutter, cut the butter and mix till a crumbly mixture forms.
6. Place the mixture over the apple slices evenly and cook everything in the oven for about 30-40 minutes.

Elegant Apple
& Cheddar Stuffed
Chicken Breast

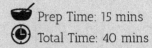 Prep Time: 15 mins

Total Time: 40 mins

Servings per Recipe: 4
Calories	139 kcal
Fat	5.1 g
Carbohydrates	4.9g
Protein	15 g
Cholesterol	46 mg
Sodium	120 mg

Ingredients

2 skinless, boneless chicken breasts
1/2 C. chopped apple
2 tbsp shredded Cheddar cheese
1 tbsp Italian-style dried bread crumbs
1 tbsp butter
1/4 C. dry white wine

1/4 C. water
1 tbsp water
1 1/2 tsp cornstarch
1 tbsp chopped fresh parsley, for garnish

Directions

1. In a bowl, mix together the apple, breadcrumbs and cheese.
2. Place the chicken breasts between 2 sheets of wax paper and with a meat mallet, flatten to 1/4-inch thickness.
3. Place the mixture in the center of the chicken breasts evenly.
4. Roll each breast around the filling and secure with the toothpicks.
5. In a large skillet, melt the butter on medium heat and cook the chicken breasts till browned completely.
6. Add the wine and 1/4 C. of the water and simmer, covered for about 15-20 minutes.
7. Transfer the chicken breasts onto a plate.
8. In a bowl, mix together the cornstarch and the remaining water.
9. Add the cornstarch mixture in the skillet with juices and cook till the gravy becomes thick.
10. Pour the gravy over the chicken breasts and serve with a garnishing of parsley.

ADORABLE
Apple Pies

Prep Time: 20 mins
Total Time: 1 hr 20 mins

Servings per Recipe: 4

Calories	614 kcal
Fat	29.9 g
Carbohydrates	83.1g
Protein	5.9 g
Cholesterol	0 mg
Sodium	469 mg

Ingredients

2 pastries for 9-inch single crust pies
3 C. diced Granny Smith apple
2 tbsp instant tapioca
1/2 C. white sugar

lemon juice
1/8 tsp ground nutmeg
1/4 tsp ground cinnamon

Directions

1. Set your oven to 400 degrees F before doing anything else.
2. Cut about 4 (6-inch) rounds from the pie crusts.
3. Arrange the crust rounds into 4 (5-inch) mini pie pans.
4. Cut about 1/8-inch strips from the remaining crusts.
5. In a bowl, mix together the remaining ingredients and keep aside for about 5 minutes.
6. Stir the mixture well and divide it between the pie shells evenly.
7. Arrange the pie strips over each pie and pinch the strips onto the bottom crust.
8. Cook everything in the oven for about 30 minutes.

Addicting
Apple Snack

Prep Time: 15 mins
Total Time: 55 mins

Servings per Recipe: 9
Calories   328 kcal
Fat   19.4 g
Carbohydrates   36.8g
Protein   4.3 g
Cholesterol   48 mg
Sodium   151 mg

Ingredients

1/2 C. melted butter
1 C. white sugar
1 egg
1 C. all-purpose flour
1/2 tsp baking soda
1 tsp ground cinnamon

1 C. apples - peeled, cored and finely diced
1 C. chopped walnuts

Directions

1. Set your oven to 350 degrees F before doing anything else and grease and flour an 8x8-inch baking dish.
2. In a large bowl, mix together the butter, egg and sugar.
3. Add the flour, baking soda and cinnamon and mix till well combined.
4. Fold in the apples and walnuts and transfer the mixture onto the prepared baking dish evenly.
5. Cook everything in the oven for about 40 minutes.

OUTSTANDING
Apple Dessert

Prep Time: 30 mins
Total Time: 1 hr 15 mins

Servings per Recipe: 20
Calories	377 kcal
Fat	14.6 g
Carbohydrates	59.8g
Protein	3.5 g
Cholesterol	21 mg
Sodium	240 mg

Ingredients

2 tsp salt
4 C. all-purpose flour
1 1/3 C. shortening
2 egg yolks, beaten
1/2 C. milk
10 apples - peeled, cored and sliced

2 tbsp all-purpose flour
3 C. white sugar
1 tbsp ground cinnamon
1 egg white

Directions

1. Set your oven to 375 degrees F before doing anything else and grease a 15x10-inch jelly roll pan.
2. In a large bowl, add 4 C. of the flour and salt.
3. With a pastry cutter, cut the shortening and mix till a crumbly mixture forms.
4. Add the milk and egg yolks and mix till a dough forms.
5. Divide the dough into 2 portions and place one part of the dough onto a lightly floured surface.
6. With a rolling pin, roll the dough into a 1/8-inch thickness.
7. Arrange the rolled dough portion in the bottom of the prepared pan.
8. Place the apple slices over the crust evenly.
9. In a bowl, mix together 2 tbsp of the flour, cinnamon and sugar and sprinkle everything over the apple slices evenly.
10. Now, roll the remaining dough portions and place everything over the apple slices.
11. With your hands, pinch the ends to seal and trim the excess crust.
12. Coat with the egg white evenly and cook everything in the oven for about 40-45 minutes.
13. Remove everything from the oven and keep aside to cool completely.
14. With a sharp knife cut into desired squares and serve.

Blonde
Apple Brownies

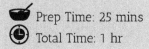 Prep Time: 25 mins
Total Time: 1 hr

Servings per Recipe: 12
Calories	227 kcal
Fat	11.5 g
Carbohydrates	30.3g
Protein	2.5 g
Cholesterol	36 mg
Sodium	177 mg

Ingredients

1/2 C. butter, melted
1 C. white sugar
1 egg
3 medium apples - peeled, cored and
thinly sliced
1/2 C. chopped walnuts

1 C. all-purpose flour
1/4 tsp salt
1/2 tsp baking powder
1/2 tsp baking soda
1 tsp ground cinnamon

Directions

1. Set your oven to 350 degrees F before doing anything else and grease and flour a 9x9-inch baking dish.
2. In a bowl, add the melted butter, egg and sugar and beat till fluffy.
3. In another bowl, sift together the flour, baking soda, baking powder, cinnamon and salt.
4. Add the egg mixture into the flour mixture and mix till well combined.
5. Fold in the apples and walnuts and transfer the mixture onto the prepared baking dish evenly.
6. Cook everything in the oven for about 35 minutes.

APPLE CAKE
in Romanian Style

Prep Time: 20 mins
Total Time: 1 hr 15 mins

Servings per Recipe: 12
Calories	393 kcal
Fat	20.1 g
Carbohydrates	50.2g
Protein	5 g
Cholesterol	46 mg
Sodium	124 mg

Ingredients

5 apples, peeled, cored and cut into
1-inch wedges
3 eggs
1 1/2 C. white sugar
3/4 C. vegetable oil
1 tsp baking soda

1 tsp ground cinnamon
1 tbsp vanilla extract
2 C. all-purpose flour
3/4 C. chopped walnuts

Directions

1. Set your oven to 350 degrees F before doing anything else and grease and flour a 13x9-inch baking dish.
2. In a large bowl, add the sugar and eggs and beat till well combined.
3. Add the flour, baking soda, cinnamon, oil and vanilla and mix till well combined.
4. Fold in the apples and walnuts and transfer the mixture onto the prepared baking dish evenly.
5. Cook everything in the oven for about 55 minutes.

Crunchy
Apple Cobbler

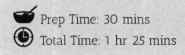 Prep Time: 30 mins

Total Time: 1 hr 25 mins

Servings per Recipe: 8

Calories	404 kcal
Fat	17.1 g
Carbohydrates	61.4g
Protein	4.7 g
Cholesterol	48 mg
Sodium	214 mg

Ingredients

4 C. thinly sliced apples
1/2 C. white sugar
1/2 tsp ground cinnamon
1/2 C. chopped pecans
1 C. all-purpose flour
1 C. white sugar
1 tsp baking powder
1/4 tsp salt

1 egg, beaten
1/2 C. evaporated milk
1/3 C. butter, melted
1/4 C. chopped pecans

Directions

1. Set your oven to 325 degrees F before doing anything else and grease a large baking dish.
2. In the bottom of the prepared baking dish, place the apple slices in a single layer.
3. In a bowl, mix together the 1/2 C. of the pecans, 1/2 C. of the sugar and cinnamon and spread everything over the apple slices.
4. In a second bowl, mix together the flour, baking powder, 1 C. of the sugar and salt.
5. In a third bowl, add the evaporated milk, egg and melted butter and beat till well combined.
6. Add the egg mixture into the flour mixture and mix till well combined.
7. Place the flour mixture over the apples and sprinkle everything with the remaining pecans evenly.
8. Cook everything in the oven for about 55 minutes.

NUTRITIOUS
Apple Cobbler

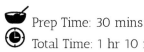

Prep Time: 30 mins
Total Time: 1 hr 10 mins

Servings per Recipe: 15

Calories	294 kcal
Fat	8 g
Carbohydrates	54.6g
Protein	3.2 g
Cholesterol	32 mg
Sodium	164 mg

Ingredients

3 large Granny Smith apples, peeled
and sliced
3/4 C. white sugar
2 tbsp ground cinnamon
1 tsp ground nutmeg
2 tbsp lemon juice
1/4 C. butter, softened
3/4 C. white sugar
1 egg
2 C. all-purpose flour
2 tsp baking powder

1/4 tsp salt
1/2 C. milk
2 C. fresh blueberries
2/3 C. white sugar
1/2 C. all-purpose flour
1 tsp ground cinnamon
1/3 C. cold butter

Directions

1. Set your oven to 375 degrees F before doing anything else and lightly, grease a 13x9-inch baking dish.
2. In a bowl, add the apples, lemon juice, 3/4 C. of the sugar, 2 tbsp of the cinnamon and nutmeg and toss to coat well.
3. Refrigerate, covered till ready for serving.
4. In a bowl, add the softened butter and 3/4 C. of the sugar and beat till smooth and creamy.
5. Add the eggs and beat till well combined.
6. In another bowl, mix together 2 C. of the flour, baking powder and salt.
7. Add the egg mixture into the flour mixture and mix till well combined.
8. Fold in the blueberries.
9. In the bottom of the prepared baking dish, place the apple slices in a single layer and top with the blueberry mixture evenly.

10. In a third bowl, mix together the remaining flour, sugar and cinnamon.

11. With a pastry cutter, cut the butter and mix till a crumbly mixture forms.

12. Spread the mixture over the blueberry mixture evenly and cook everything in the oven for about 40 - 45 minutes.

APPLE CAKE
in Old-English Style

Prep Time: 15 mins
Total Time: 1 hr

Servings per Recipe: 8
Calories	295 kcal
Fat	6.4 g
Carbohydrates	56.6g
Protein	4.8 g
Cholesterol	11 mg
Sodium	419 mg

Ingredients

1 tbsp butter, melted
1 (1 lb.) loaf white bread, crusts trimmed
8 apples - peeled, cored and chopped
1/3 C. white sugar
1/2 tbsp ground cinnamon

1 tbsp lemon juice
2 tbsp butter, cubed
nonstick cooking spray

Directions

1. Set your oven to 400 degrees F before doing anything else and grease a 9x5-inch loaf pan with melted butter.
2. Arrange the required bread slices in the bottom and the sides of the prepared loaf pan evenly.
3. In a bowl, mix together the remaining ingredients and place over the bread slices.
4. Cover the apple mixture with the remaining bread slices and drizzle with the cooking spray.
5. Cover with a sheet of foil and cook everything in the oven for about 35-40 minutes.
6. Remove everything from the oven and keep aside for about 15 minutes to cool.

Spectacular
Apple & Cheese Casserole

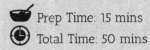 Prep Time: 15 mins
Total Time: 50 mins

Servings per Recipe: 12
Calories	249 kcal
Fat	12.6 g
Carbohydrates	30.5g
Protein	4.7 g
Cholesterol	32 mg
Sodium	239 mg

Ingredients

1 C. white sugar
1/2 C. butter, softened
1/2 lb. processed cheese food, cut into small chunks

3/4 C. all-purpose flour
1 (16 oz.) can sliced apples, undrained

Directions

1. Set your oven to 350 degrees F before doing anything else.
2. In a bowl, add the butter and sugar and beat till smooth and creamy.
3. Add the flour and beat till well combined.
4. Fold in the cheese.
5. In the bottom of a 13x9-inch baking dish, arrange the apple slices.
6. Place the cheese mixture over the apple slices evenly.
7. Cook everything in the oven for about 35-40 minutes.

SUMMERTIME
Apple Salad

Prep Time: 30 mins
Total Time: 30 mins

Servings per Recipe: 8

Calories	98 kcal
Fat	3.6 g
Carbohydrates	16.8g
Protein	1.2 g
Cholesterol	0 mg
Sodium	64 mg

Ingredients

2 C. shredded napa cabbage
1 (1 lb.) jicama, peeled and shredded
2 C. shredded daikon radish
2 Granny Smith apples - peeled, cored
and shredded
2 large carrots, shredded
1 firm pear, shredded

1/4 C. finely chopped cilantro
2 tbsp olive oil
3 tbsp orange juice
1 tbsp lime juice
sea salt and pepper to taste

Directions

1. In a large bowl, add all the ingredients and toss to coat well.
2. Serve immediately.

Autumn
Apple Salad

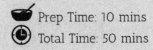 Prep Time: 10 mins

Total Time: 50 mins

Servings per Recipe: 2

Calories	129 kcal
Fat	0.3 g
Carbohydrates	34.2g
Protein	1.2 g
Cholesterol	0 mg
Sodium	197 mg

Ingredients

3 tbsp raisins
2 tart apples, peeled and shredded
1 C. shredded pumpkin
2 tsp lemon juice

salt and pepper to taste

Directions

1. In a bowl of hot water, soak the raisins and keep aside, covered for about 30 minutes.
2. Drain well and transfer into a large bowl.
3. Add the remaining ingredients and toss to coat well.
4. Serve immediately.

ASIAN
Apple Slaw

Prep Time: 25 mins
Total Time: 1 hr 5 mins

Servings per Recipe: 6

Calories	282 kcal
Fat	20.6 g
Carbohydrates	23.1g
Protein	5.3 g
Cholesterol	0 mg
Sodium	536 mg

Ingredients

6 tbsp rice wine vinegar
6 tbsp olive oil
5 tbsp creamy peanut butter
3 tbsp soy sauce
3 tbsp brown sugar
2 tbsp minced fresh ginger root
1 1/2 tbsp minced garlic

1/2 head red cabbage, finely shredded
2 Fuji apples - peeled, cored, and finely diced
1/4 C. finely minced white onion

Directions

1. In a large bowl, mix together the apples, cabbage and onion.
2. In another bowl, add the remaining ingredients and beat till well combined and smooth.
3. Pour the dressing over salad and toss to coat well.
4. Refrigerate to chill before serving.

Unique
Flavored Apple Cookies

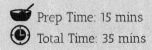 Prep Time: 15 mins

Total Time: 35 mins

Servings per Recipe: 12

Calories	237 kcal
Fat	15.2 g
Carbohydrates	23.3g
Protein	3.6 g
Cholesterol	37 mg
Sodium	52 mg

Ingredients

1/2 C. unsalted butter
1 egg yolk
1 C. chopped pecans
3/4 tsp vanilla extract
1/2 C. white sugar
1 C. all-purpose flour

1/2 C. toasted wheat germ
1/4 tsp salt
1/3 C. apple butter

Directions

1. Set your oven to 350 degrees F before doing anything else.
2. In a bowl, add the butter, egg whites and vanilla extract and beat till smooth and creamy.
3. In a food processor, add the pecans and sugar and pulse till a fine texture forms.
4. Add the flour, wheat germ and salt and pulse till well combined.
5. Add the flour mixture into the butter mixture and mix till a dough forms.
6. Make 1-inch balls from the dough and arrange onto the cookie sheets in a single layer about 2-inches apart.
7. With your thumbs, create a dent on the top of each ball.
8. Cook everything in the oven for about 15-20 minutes.
9. Remove everything from the oven and with a spoon, open the vents.
10. Keep on wire racks to cool completely.
11. Fill each vent with the apple butter and serve.

CHEWY
Apple Cookies

Prep Time: 20 mins
Total Time: 40 mins

Servings per Recipe: 36
Calories	90 kcal
Fat	5.4 g
Carbohydrates	9.4g
Protein	1.5 g
Cholesterol	10 mg
Sodium	50 mg

Ingredients

1 C. sifted all-purpose flour
1 tsp baking powder
1/2 tsp salt
1 tsp ground cinnamon
1/2 tsp ground nutmeg
1/2 C. shortening
3/4 C. white sugar

2 eggs
1 C. chopped walnuts
1 C. apples - peeled, cored and finely diced
1 C. rolled oats

Directions

1. Set your oven to 350 degrees F before doing anything else.
2. In a large bowl, mix together the flour, baking powder, cinnamon, nutmeg and salt.
3. In another bowl, add the shortening and white sugar and beat till smooth and creamy.
4. Add the eggs and beat till well combined.
5. Add the egg mixture into the flour mixture and mix till well combined.
6. Fold in the oats, apples and walnuts.
7. With a spoon, place the mixture onto the cookie sheets in a single layer about 2-inches apart.
8. Cook everything in the oven for about 12-15 minutes.
9. Remove everything from the oven and keep it all on wire racks to cool completely.

Home-Style
Apple Dessert

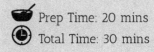

Prep Time: 20 mins
Total Time: 30 mins

Servings per Recipe: 8

Calories	346 kcal
Fat	12.4 g
Carbohydrates	57.6 g
Protein	3 g
Cholesterol	31 mg
Sodium	106 mg

Ingredients

1 C. all-purpose flour
3/4 C. packed brown sugar
1/2 C. rolled oats
1/4 C. graham cracker crumbs
1 tsp ground cinnamon
1/2 C. melted butter
3 1/2 C. peeled and sliced apples
1 1/2 C. blueberries

1 tbsp lemon juice
1/4 C. white sugar
2 tbsp cornstarch
1 C. cold water
1 tsp vanilla extract

Directions

1. Grease a large microwave safe casserole dish.
2. In a large bowl, mix together the flour, oats, brown sugar, crackers and cinnamon.
3. Add the butter and mix till well combined.
4. Place half of the flour mixture in the bottom of the prepared casserole dish evenly.
5. Place the apples and blueberries over the flour mixture evenly and drizzle with the lemon juice.
6. In a microwave safe bowl, mix together cornstarch, white sugar, vanilla extract and water.
7. Microwave on high for about 2-4 minutes, stirring every 45 seconds.
8. Pour the cornstarch mixture over the fruit layer evenly and top with the remaining flour mixture.
9. Cook everything in the oven for about 25 minutes.
10. Remove everything from the oven and keep aside to cool slightly.

FESTIVE
Apple Treat

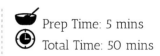 Prep Time: 5 mins
Total Time: 50 mins

Servings per Recipe: 5
Calories	831 kcal
Fat	34.8 g
Carbohydrates	131.6 g
Protein	8.1 g
Cholesterol	22 mg
Sodium	249 mg

Ingredients

5 large Granny Smith apples
wooden craft sticks
1 (14 oz.) package individually wrapped
caramels, unwrapped
2 tbsp water
7 oz. chocolate candy bar, broken into
pieces

2 tbsp shortening, divided
1 C. colored candy coating melts

Directions

1. In a large pan of boiling water, dip the apples for a while.
2. With a slotted spoon remove everything from the water and pat them dry.
3. Line a cookie sheet with greased foil.
4. In the core of each apple, insert a wooden stick at the stem end.
5. Arrange the apples onto the prepared cookie sheet.
6. In a microwave safe bowl, add the caramel and water and microwave on high for about 2 minutes.
7. Stir well and microwave on high till melted completely, stirring every 1 minute.
8. Dip the apples in the caramel mixture evenly.
9. In a microwave safe bowl, add the chocolate candy bar and 1 tbsp of the shortening and microwave on high till melted completely.
10. Dip the apples in the chocolate mixture evenly.
11. In a microwave safe bowl, add the candy coating and the remaining shortening and microwave on high till melted completely, stirring every 30 seconds.
12. Dip a fork in the coating mixture and make designs on apples and refrigerate till set.

Crunchy Apples

Prep Time: 25 mins
Total Time: 35 mins

Servings per Recipe: 6

Calories	704 kcal
Fat	25.3 g
Carbohydrates	116g
Protein	9.5 g
Cholesterol	13 mg
Sodium	341 mg

Ingredients

6 Granny Smith apples
6 wooden sticks
1 (14 oz.) package individually wrapped caramels, unwrapped
2 tbsp water
1/2 tsp vanilla extract
3 C. chopped peanut butter filled sandwich cookies

4 oz. milk chocolate, chopped
4 oz. white chocolate, chopped

Directions

1. Line a cookie sheet with greased foil.
2. In the core of each apple, insert a wooden stick at the stem end.
3. Arrange the apples onto the prepared cookie sheet.
4. In a pan, mix together the water and caramel on low heat.
5. Cook, stirring occasionally till caramel are melted completely.
6. Stir in the vanilla extract and remove from the heat.
7. Dip the apples in the caramel mixture evenly.
8. In a shallow dish, place the cookies.
9. Roll the apples into cookies evenly and arrange onto the cookie sheet.
10. In 2 microwave safe bowl, add both the chocolate chips separately and microwave on high till melted completely, stirring every 30 seconds.
11. Pour the melted milk chocolate over apples, followed by the white chocolate chips and refrigerate till set.

SENSATIONAL
Apples

Prep Time: 15 mins
Total Time: 30 mins

Servings per Recipe: 6

Calories	445 kcal
Fat	13.7 g
Carbohydrates	85.1g
Protein	4.6 g
Cholesterol	5 mg
Sodium	1485 mg

Ingredients

6 Granny Smith apples
6 wooden sticks
1 (14 oz.) package individually wrapped
caramels, unwrapped
2 tbsp water
1/2 tsp vanilla extract

1 1/2 tbsp coarse sea salt
1 C. semisweet chocolate chips

Directions

1. Line a cookie sheet with greased foil.
2. In the core of each apple, insert a wooden stick at the stem end.
3. Arrange the apples onto the prepared cookie sheet.
4. In a pan, mix together the water and caramel on low heat.
5. Cook, stirring occasionally till the caramel is melted completely.
6. Stir in the vanilla extract and remove from the heat.
7. Dip the apples in the caramel mixture evenly and arrange onto the cookie sheet.
8. Sprinkle with the salt and refrigerate to chill.
9. In a microwave safe bowl, add the chocolate chips and microwave on high till melted completely, stirring every 30 seconds.
10. Pour the melted chocolate over the apples and refrigerate till everything is set.

Old-Timed
Baked Apples

🥣 Prep Time: 15 mins
🕐 Total Time: 30 mins

Servings per Recipe: 4
Calories   270 kcal
Fat   11.5 g
Carbohydrates   45g
Protein   0.6 g
Cholesterol   31 mg
Sodium   91 mg

Ingredients

4 tart green apples
1/2 C. brown sugar
4 tbsp butter

2 tsp ground cinnamon

Directions

1. Set your oven to 350 degrees F before doing anything else.
2. Scoop out the core of each apple from the top, leaving a well.
3. Fill each apple well with 2 tbsp of the brown sugar and 1 tbsp of the butter.
4. In a shallow baking dish, arrange the apples and sprinkle them with the cinnamon evenly.
5. Cook everything in the oven for about 15 minutes.

APPLE TREAT
for Chocolate Lovers

Prep Time: 30 mins
Total Time: 1 hr 30 mins

Servings per Recipe: 10
Calories	589 kcal
Fat	34.6 g
Carbohydrates	73.3g
Protein	8.9 g
Cholesterol	1 mg
Sodium	67 mg

Ingredients

10 small Granny Smith apples
1/2 C. chopped roasted peanuts
1/2 C. candy-coated milk chocolate candies

2 lb. semisweet chocolate, chopped

Directions

1. In the core of each apple, insert a lollipop stick at the stem end.
2. In 2 shallow dishes, place the peanuts and candies separately.
3. In a pan of simmering water, arrange a heatproof glass bowl.
4. Add the chocolate chips and stir continuously till everything melts completely.
5. Coat the apples with the melted chocolate evenly and roll them in the peanuts followed by the candies.
6. Place the apples on a wax paper lined baking sheet and keep aside for about 20 minutes.

Deep South
Fried Maple Apples

Prep Time: 10 mins
Total Time: 20 mins

Servings per Recipe: 4
Calories	263 kcal
Fat	14.1 g
Carbohydrates	37.5g
Protein	0.4 g
Cholesterol	0 mg
Sodium	111 mg

Ingredients

5 apples - peeled, cored and sliced
1/4 C. vegetable oil
1/4 C. maple flavored syrup

1 pinch salt

Directions

1. In a cast iron pan, heat the oil on medium heat and cook the apple slices till soft on both sides.
2. Sprinkle everything with salt and drizzle the maple syrup over everything.

APPLE SOUP
For Cold Fall Nights

 Prep Time: 20 mins
Total Time: 1 hr

Servings per Recipe: 7

Calories	102 kcal
Fat	1.3 g
Carbohydrates	22.9 g
Protein	1.2 g
Cholesterol	0 mg
Sodium	349 mg

Ingredients

1 tbsp reduced-fat margarine
3 tart apples - peeled, cored, and chopped
3 pears - peeled, cored, and chopped
5 C. vegetable broth
1/2 tsp rubbed sage
1/4 tsp ground black pepper

1 bay leaf
1 1/2 tsp pureed fresh ginger
1 tbsp chopped fresh parsley

Directions

1. In a large pan, melt the margarine on medium heat and cook the apples and peas for about 5 minutes.
2. Add the broth, sage, bay leaf and pepper and bring everything to a boil.
3. Reduce the heat to low and simmer, covered for about 20 minutes.
4. Remove everything from the heat and keep aside for about 5 minutes to cool.
5. In a blender, add the soup mixture in batches and pulse till smooth.
6. Return the soup in the pan on medium heat and cook till heated completely.
7. Serve with a topping of parsley.

Irresistibly
Crispy Apple Pancakes

Prep Time: 20 mins
Total Time: 40 mins

Servings per Recipe: 5
Calories   178 kcal
Fat   4.7 g
Carbohydrates   29.4g
Protein   5.7 g
Cholesterol   75 mg
Sodium   69 mg

Ingredients

3 russet potatoes, peeled and shredded
1 Granny Smith apple - peeled, cored, and shredded
2 eggs
2 tbsp all-purpose flour
3 green onions, diced

salt to taste
vegetable oil for frying, or as needed
1/2 tbsp sour cream

Directions

1. Squeeze the apple and potato to drain the excess moisture.
2. In a bowl, mix together the apple, potatoes, green onion, flour and eggs.
3. In a large heavy skillet, heat the oil on medium-high heat.
4. Divide the mixture into palm sized patties and cook everything for about 2-4 minutes per side. (Cook the dish in batches).
5. Transfer the pancakes onto a paper towel lined plate and sprinkle with the salt.
6. Serve with a topping of the sour cream.

IRISH
Apple Mash

Prep Time: 15 mins
Total Time: 50 mins

Servings per Recipe: 6
Calories	293 kcal
Fat	8.9 g
Carbohydrates	51g
Protein	5.6 g
Cholesterol	25 mg
Sodium	457 mg

Ingredients

2 C. water, divided
1 tsp brown sugar
1 small lemon, halved and juiced, halves reserved
1 large apple (such as Honey Crisp), peeled and chopped
4 large baking potatoes, peeled and chopped

6 C. water
3 tbsp butter
3 tbsp heavy whipping cream
1 tsp salt
1 tbsp ground black pepper

Directions

1. In a pan, mix together the apple, reserved lemon halves, brown sugar, lemon juice and 2 C. of the water on medium-high heat.
2. Boil for about 10-12 minutes and drain well, then transfer into a large bowl.
3. Discard the lemon halves and keep the apple slices warm by covering them with foil.
4. In a large pan, add the potatoes and 6 C. of the water on medium-high heat.
5. Cook everything for 15-20 minutes and drain well.
6. Add the potatoes in the bowl with the apple and with a hand blender mash them completely.

Thanksgiving
Favorite Apple Dessert

🥣 Prep Time: 10 mins
🕐 Total Time: 30 mins

Servings per Recipe: 8
Calories   153 kcal
Fat   3.1 g
Carbohydrates   30.7g
Protein   2 g
Cholesterol   8 mg
Sodium   84 mg

Ingredients

2 large sweet potatoes, peeled and diced
2 large Honeycrisp apples, diced
2 tsp ground cinnamon
1/2 tsp ground nutmeg

2/3 C. water
2 tbsp butter, diced

Directions

1. Set your oven to 425 degrees F before doing anything else.
2. In the bottom of a microwave safe loaf pan, arrange the sweet potatoes and apples and sprinkle them with nutmeg and cinnamon.
3. Add enough water to cover about 1/2-inch of the bottom and cook everything in the microwave for about 8 minutes.
4. Drain well.
5. Place the butter over the apple mixture in the shape of dots and cook everything in the oven for about 10 minutes.

REFRESHING
Apple Juice

Prep Time: 10 mins
Total Time: 10 mins

Servings per Recipe: 1

Calories	277 kcal
Fat	1.3 g
Carbohydrates	68.6g
Protein	4 g
Cholesterol	0 mg
Sodium	266 mg

Ingredients

4 carrots, trimmed
2 apples, quartered
2 stalks celery

1 (1/2 inch) piece fresh ginger

Directions

1. In a juicer, add all the ingredients except the ginger and process according to manufacturer's directions.
2. Add the ginger and process again.

Traditional
Autumn Sweet Treat

Prep Time: 35 mins
Total Time: 1 hr

Servings per Recipe: 8

Calories	298 kcal
Fat	6.5 g
Carbohydrates	60.7g
Protein	2.5 g
Cholesterol	15 mg
Sodium	49 mg

Ingredients

4 1/2 C. peeled, cored and sliced apples
2 tsp lemon juice
2 tbsp water
3/4 C. brown sugar

3/4 C. all-purpose flour
3/4 C. rolled oats
4 tbsp butter

Directions

1. Set your oven to 350 degrees F before doing anything else and lightly, grease a casserole dish.
2. Place the apple slices in the bottom of the prepared casserole dish evenly.
3. In a bowl, mix together the water and lemon juice and drizzle over the apple slices evenly.
4. In another bowl, add the remaining ingredients and mix till a coarse crumb forms.
5. Spread the crumb mixture over the apple slices evenly and cook everything in the oven for about 25 minutes.

AWESOME
Apple Glaze for Ham

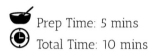

Prep Time: 5 mins
Total Time: 10 mins

Servings per Recipe: 12

Calories	47 kcal
Fat	0.1 g
Carbohydrates	11.6g
Protein	0.2 g
Cholesterol	0 mg
Sodium	18 mg

Ingredients

1 C. apple butter
1/2 C. orange juice
1 tbsp dried onion flakes

1 tbsp Worcestershire sauce

Directions

1. In a pan, add all the ingredients and simmer till thickened.

Family
Favorite Apple Spread

Prep Time: 5 mins
Total Time: 45 mins

Servings per Recipe: 12
Calories	65 kcal
Fat	3.4 g
Carbohydrates	6.4g
Protein	2.1 g
Cholesterol	11 mg
Sodium	58 mg

Ingredients

1 (8 oz.) package light cream cheese, softened
1/2 C. apple butter
1/2 tsp vanilla extract

1 pinch ground cinnamon

Directions

1. In a food processor, add the apple butter, cream cheese, vanilla and cinnamon and pulse till smooth.
2. Transfer the mixture into a bowl and refrigerate, covered for about 30 minutes.

APPLE BRINE
for Thanksgiving

Prep Time: 15 mins
Total Time: 1 hr 45 mins

Servings per Recipe: 1
Calories	1964 kcal
Fat	8.2 g
Carbohydrates	484.3g
Protein	15.3 g
Cholesterol	0 mg
Sodium	1849 mg

Ingredients

1/4 C. dried rosemary
1/4 C. ground thyme
2 tbsp rubbed sage
4 bay leaves
1 tsp ground black pepper

1 gallon boiling water
1 lb. kosher salt
1 gallon cold apple juice

Directions

1. In a cloth spice bag, add the herbs, bay leaves and black pepper.
2. In a large pan, add the water and salt and mix till the salt is dissolved completely.
3. Bring everything to a boil and add the spice bag and simmer for about 20 minutes.
4. Remove everything from the heat and keep aside for about 1 hour to cool completely.
5. Stir in the cold apple juice.

Japanese
Fruity Chicken Curry

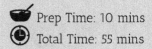 Prep Time: 10 mins

Total Time: 55 mins

Servings per Recipe: 4

Calories	420.5
Fat	17.9g
Cholesterol	101.1mg
Sodium	734.0mg
Carbohydrates	33.1g
Protein	31.9g

Ingredients

3 C. chicken stock
1 tbsp canola oil
1 lb boneless skinless chicken, cut into chunks
salt and pepper
3 tbsp butter
1 tsp fresh ginger, finely chopped
1/2 medium onion, finely chopped
1/2 medium onion, cut into 1-inch chunks
1 garlic clove, finely chopped
3 tbsp flour

2 tbsp curry powder
2 tbsp crushed tomatoes
1 bay leaf
1 medium carrot, chopped to 1/2-inch pieces
1 medium potato, chopped in 1-inch pieces
1 small fuji apple, grated
1 tsp honey
1 tbsp soy sauce

Directions

1. Place a medium saucepan over medium heat: Pour the stock in it and heat it through. Sprinkle some salt and pepper on the chicken.
2. Place a large wok over medium heat: Heat the oil in it. Add the chicken pieces and cook them for 5 min on each side. Drain it and place it aside.
3. Add the butter to the wok and heat it until it melts. Cook in it the ginger, garlic, and chopped onion for 4 min.
4. Add the flour and cook them for 2 min. Stir in 1/2 C. of hot stock and mix them well.
5. Stir in the tomato with curry. Transfer the mix to the pot with the remaining hot stock.
6. Stir in the chicken, onion, potato, and carrot. Cook the curry until it starts simmering. Cook it for 32 min. Stir in the apples, soy sauce, and honey.
7. Cook the curry for 6 min. Serve it warm with some rice.
8. Enjoy.

SKYTOP
PB Wraps

Prep Time: 10 mins
Total Time: 15 mins

Servings per Recipe: 4
Calories	332.7
Fat	16.5g
Cholesterol	0.0mg
Sodium	412.4mg
Carbohydrates	37.7g
Protein	10.6g

Ingredients

4 (7 - 8 inch) flour tortillas
1/3 C. peanut butter
1 C. chopped granny smith apple

1/4 C. oats & honey granola cereal

Directions

1. Place the tortillas on a cutting board. Coat one side of them with peanut butter.
2. Microwave each tortilla for 10 sec. Transfer to a serving plate.
3. Top them with chopped apple and cereal. Roll them rightly.
4. Serve your wraps right away with extra toppings of your choice.
5. Enjoy.

Whole Wheat
Apple Wraps

Prep Time: 25 mins
Total Time: 42 mins

Servings per Recipe: 2
Calories   768.0
Fat   17.1g
Cholesterol   31.4mg
Sodium   736.7mg
Carbohydrates   143.3g
Protein   16.1g

Ingredients

2 C. peeled cored and diced tart green apples
1/4 C. raisins
1/4 C. honey
1 tsp ground cinnamon
1/8 tsp salt
1 tbsp butter

1 1/3 C. whole milk
1 C. rolled oats
1 tsp vanilla extract
1/4 C. apple butter
2 10 inch whole wheat tortillas

Directions

1. Get a mixing bowl: Combine in it the apples with raisins, honey, cinnamon, and salt.
2. Place a pan over medium heat. Heat in it the butter.
3. Stir in it the honey apple mixture and let them cook for 9 min.
4. Stir in the milk with oatmeal. Let them cook for an extra 6 min over low heat.
5. Turn off the heat and stir in the vanilla extract.
6. Place the tortillas on a cutting board. Spread the apple mixture over them then roll them.
7. Slice your wraps in half then serve them.
8. Enjoy.

WENDY'S
Lunch Box (Honey Cheddar on Whole Grain)

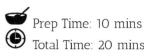

Prep Time: 10 mins
Total Time: 20 mins

Servings per Recipe: 4	
Calories	445.5
Fat	22.3g
Cholesterol	59.6mg
Sodium	752.9mg
Carbohydrates	40.8g
Protein	21.7g

Ingredients

8 slices whole grain bread
1/4 C. honey mustard
2 crisp apples, sliced

8 oz. mild cheddar cheese, sliced
cooking spray

Directions

1. Set your panini press as suggested by the manual and lightly, grease with the cooking spray.
2. Place a thin layer of the honey mustard onto all bread slices evenly.
3. Place the apple slices onto 4 bread slices, followed by the cheese.
4. Cover with the remaining bread slices.
5. Place the sandwiches into panini press and cook for about 3-5 minutes.
6. Enjoy warm.

Apple
& Carrot Stir Fry

Prep Time: 5 mins
Total Time: 15 mins

Servings per Recipe: 2
Calories	705.2
Fat	34.9g
Cholesterol	0.0mg
Sodium	357.4mg
Carbohydrates	88.9g
Protein	15.9g

Ingredients

2 granny smith apples, cored and diced
1 C. sliced carrot
1 C. snow peas
1/3 C. dry roasted salted peanut
2 tbsp canola oil

1 tbsp basil
2 C. cooked brown rice (steamed)
soy sauce (optional)

Directions

1. In a large skillet, heat the oil on medium heat and sauté the peanuts, carrots and basil for about 5 minutes.
2. Stir in the snow peas and cook for about 5 minutes, stirring frequently.
3. Stir in the apples and soy sauce and remove from the heat.
4. Serve hot over the steamed rice.

SWEET
Carolina Apple Quesadillas

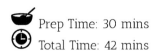 Prep Time: 30 mins
Total Time: 42 mins

Servings per Recipe: 6
Calories   679.2
Fat   38.8g
Cholesterol   77.4mg
Sodium   750.6mg
Carbohydrates   76.9g
Protein   10.1g

Ingredients

2 granny smith apples, sliced
1/2 C. dried sweetened cranberries
1 tsp cinnamon sugar
1 tsp lemon juice
7 tbsp butter, divided
6 10-inch flour tortillas

1 (8 oz.) packages cream cheese, softened
1/4 C. powdered sugar
1/2 C. caramel sauce
1/2 C. chopped pecans, toasted

Directions

1. In a bowl, add the apples, cranberries, cinnamon sugar and lemon juice and toss to coat well.
2. In a nonstick skillet, a 1 tbsp of the butter over medium heat and cook until melted.
3. Add the apple mixture and stir fry for about 4-5 minutes.
4. With a slotted spoon, place the apple mixture into a bowl.
5. In a bowl, add the powdered sugar and cream cheese and beat until smooth.
6. Place 1 tbsp of the butter onto 1 side of all tortillas evenly.
7. Place the cream cheese mixture onto another side of all tortillas evenly, followed by the apple mixture.
8. Carefully, fold each tortilla in half over the filling.
9. Place a skillet over medium heat until heated through.
10. Place the quesadillas and cook for about 4 minutes, flipping once half way through.
11. Transfer the quesadillas onto a platter and drizzle with the caramel sauce.
12. Enjoy with a topping of the pecans.

Dorm Room
Fruit Quesadillas

🥣 Prep Time: 10 mins
🕐 Total Time: 25 mins

Servings per Recipe: 4
Calories	661.1
Fat	38.7g
Cholesterol	104.7mg
Sodium	1267.6mg
Carbohydrates	51.6g
Protein	28.1g

Ingredients

6 whole wheat tortillas
12 oz. cheddar cheese, shredded
2 apples, washed and sliced
2 tbsp butter

1 - 2 tbsp butter

Directions

1. Place 3 tbsp of the cheese over one half of each tortilla, followed by the apple slices and 2 tbsp of the cheese.
2. Carefully, fold each tortilla in half over the filling.
3. In a skillet, add the butter over medium-high heat and cook until melted.
4. Place the quesadillas, 1 at a time and cook until golden brown from both sides.
5. Enjoy warm.

BROOKLYN
Cheesecake Quesadillas

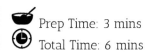

Prep Time: 3 mins
Total Time: 6 mins

Servings per Recipe: 4
Calories	336.6
Fat	21.8g
Cholesterol	62.4mg
Sodium	373.6mg
Carbohydrates	30.3g
Protein	5.9g

Ingredients

4 flour tortillas
8 oz. cream cheese, soft
2 tbsp sugar
1/4 tsp vanilla
1/4 cinnamon
1 apple, sliced

butter
cinnamon-sugar mixture

Directions

1. In a bowl, add the sugar, cream cheese, cinnamon and vanilla and cinnamon beat until creamy.
2. Place the cream cheese mixture onto half of each tortilla, followed by the apples.
3. Carefully, fold each tortilla in half over the filling.
4. In a skillet, add a little butter and cook until melted.
5. Add the quesadillas, 1 at a time and cook
6. until golden brown from both sides.
7. Transfer the quesadillas onto a platter and dust with the cinnamon sugar.
8. Cut each quesadilla into wedges and enjoy.

Apple
and Turkey Sandwiches

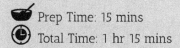

Prep Time: 15 mins
Total Time: 1 hr 15 mins

Servings per Recipe: 4

Calories	259.9
Fat	7.7g
Cholesterol	27.9mg
Sodium	277.3mg
Carbohydrates	33.1g
Protein	15.6g

Ingredients

1 C. cooked turkey, cubed
1/2 C. celery, diced
1 small Red Delicious apple, cored and cubed
2 tbsp walnuts, chopped
1 tbsp reduced-calorie mayonnaise

1 tbsp plain fat-free yogurt
1/8 tsp nutmeg
1/8 tsp cinnamon
4 lettuce leaves
8 slices raisin bread

Directions

1. In a bowl, add the yogurt, mayonnaise, turkey, apple, celery, walnuts, cinnamon and nutmeg and mix until well combined.
2. Cover the bowl and place in the fridge 8-12 hours.
3. Place 1 lettuce leaf onto each of 4 bread slices, followed by the turkey mixture.
4. Cover with the remaining bread slices and enjoy.

BUTTERED
Apple
Sandwiches

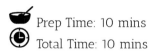 Prep Time: 10 mins

Total Time: 10 mins

Servings per Recipe: 1

Calories	293.8
Fat	15.1g
Cholesterol	33.7mg
Sodium	462.4mg
Carbohydrates	32.6g
Protein	8.4g

Ingredients

2 slices cinnamon raisin bread
1 slice American cheese
1/4 small apple, sliced

2 tsp butter, softened

Directions

1. Place the cheese slice onto 1 bread slice, followed by apple slices.
2. Top with the remaining bread slice.
3. Place the butter onto both sides of the sandwich evenly.
4. Heat a skillet over medium heat and cook the sandwich for about 2 minute per side.

Spiced
Apple Chutney

🍲 Prep Time: 1 hr
🕐 Total Time: 2 hrs 15 mins

Servings per Recipe: 10
Calories	708.1
Fat	1.7g
Cholesterol	0.0mg
Sodium	514.7mg
Carbohydrates	177.1g
Protein	4.5g

Ingredients

2 quarts chopped cored, pared tart apples
2 lbs raisins
1 C. chopped onion
1 C. chopped sweet red pepper
4 C. brown sugar
3 tbsps mustard seeds
2 tbsps ground ginger

2 tsps ground allspice
2 tsps salt
2 hot red peppers
1 garlic clove, crushed
1 quart vinegar

Directions

1. In a pan, mix together all the ingredients and simmer, stirring occasionally for about 1 hour and 15 minutes or till desired thickness of chutney.
2. Transfer the chutney into hot sterilized jars and seal tightly and place in a large bowl of boiling water for about 10 minutes.
3. (If you like mild flavored chutney than you can add 4 additional C. of apples).

GLAZED
Couscous with Maple Dressing

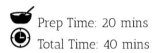

Prep Time: 20 mins
Total Time: 40 mins

Servings per Recipe: 4
Calories   687.6
Fat   29.1 g
Cholesterol   0.0 mg
Sodium   304.4 mg
Carbohydrates   89.5 g
Protein   19.1 g

Ingredients

2 tbsp. olive oil
2 C. Israeli couscous
4 C. low sodium chicken broth
1/4 C. fresh flat-leaf parsley, chopped
1 1/2 tbsp. fresh rosemary leaves, chopped
1 tsp. fresh thyme leave, chopped
1 medium green apple, diced
1 C. dried cranberries

1/2 C. slivered almonds, toasted
Dressing
1/4 C. apple cider vinegar
2 - 3 tbsp. maple syrup
1/2-1 tsp. kosher salt
1/2 tsp. fresh ground black pepper
1/4 C. olive oil

Directions

1. Place a large saucepan over high heat. Heat in it the olive oil.
2. Stir in the couscous and cook it for 4 min while stirring. Stir in the broth and cook them until they start boiling.
3. Lower the heat and let it cook for 10 to 1 min. Pour the mixture into a large bowl and let it cool down.
4. Stir in the parsley, rosemary, thyme, apple, dried cranberries, and almonds.
5. Get a mixing bowl: Whisk in it the vinegar, maple syrup, salt, and pepper.
6. Add the olive oil and mix them well. Drizzle it over the couscous and toss them to coat.
7. Adjust the seasoning of your couscous then serve it.
8. Enjoy.

Friendship Couscous

Prep Time: 10 mins
Total Time: 25 mins

Servings per Recipe: 6
Calories   306.3
Fat   9.6 g
Cholesterol   11.9 mg
Sodium   130.0 mg
Carbohydrates   45.9 g
Protein   9.2 g

Ingredients

1 zucchini, finely diced
1 tomatoes, finely diced
1 C. sweet peas
4 garlic cloves, finely chopped
2 tbsp. extra virgin olive oil
1 1/2 C. chicken stock
1 1/2 C. couscous

1 granny smith apple, finely diced
2 tbsp. of fresh mint, chopped
2 tbsp. butter
salt and pepper

Directions

1. Place a pot over high heat. Heat in it the oil.
2. Cook in it the zucchini with tomatoes, peas, and garlic for 3 min.
3. Stir in the stock and cook them until they start boiling.
4. Stir in the couscous with a pinch of salt and pepper.
5. Put on the lid and turn off the heat. Let it sit for 6 min.
6. stir it with a fork. Add the apples with mint and butter. Mix them well.
7. Serve your couscous warm or chilled.
8. Enjoy.

ADIRONDACK
Muffins

🥣 Prep Time: 25 mins
🕐 Total Time: 45 mins

Servings per Recipe: 18
Calories   271.3
Fat   13.3g
Cholesterol   27.6mg
Sodium   266.3mg
Carbohydrates   34.2g
Protein   6.0g

Ingredients

1 1/4 C. milk
1 C. granola cereal
1/2 C. brown sugar
1/2 C. melted butter
1/4 C. molasses
1 egg, beaten
1 apple, peeled and grated
2 C. flour
4 tsp baking powder

1 tsp cinnamon
1 tsp salt
1/2 C. chopped peanuts
1/2 C. raisins
1/2 C. chocolate chips
1/2 C. sunflower seeds
1/4 C. wheat germ

Directions

1. Before you do anything, preheat the oven to 400 F.
2. Get a mixing bowl: Whisk in it the milk, granola, sugar, butter, molasses, egg, and apple.
3. Get a mixing bowl: Stir in it the apple flour with baking powder, cinnamon, salt, peanut, raisins, chocolate chips, sunflower seeds, and wheat germ.
4. Add the granola mix and combine them well. Pour the mixture in a greased 18 muffin C..
5. Bake them for 18 to 20 min. Allow them to cool down completely then serve them.
6. Enjoy.

Alternative
Apple Crisps

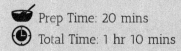 Prep Time: 20 mins
Total Time: 1 hr 10 mins

Servings per Recipe: 8
Calories	501.1
Fat	28.5g
Cholesterol	45.7mg
Sodium	168.6mg
Carbohydrates	57.2g
Protein	7.3g

Ingredients

6 medium granny smith apples, cored, peeled and sliced
1/2 C. packed brown sugar
1 tsp cinnamon

2 tbsp lemon juice
3/4 C. butter, cubed and softened
3 - 4 C. granola cereal, crushed

Directions

1. Before you do anything, preheat the oven to 400 F.
2. Get a mixing bowl: Combine in it the apples, brown sugar, lemon juice, and cinnamon.
3. Grease a baking dish with 1/3 of the butter. Arrange over it the apple slices.
4. Get a mixing bowl: Mix in it the granola with the remaining butter. Spread it over the apple layer.
5. Layover it a piece of foil to cover it. Place it in the oven and bake it for 42 to 46 min.
6. Once the time is up, discard the foil and bake it for an extra 8 to 10 min.
7. Allow the granola crumble cool down for 10 min. Serve it with some ice cream.
8. Enjoy.

35-MINUTE
Scones

Prep Time: 15 mins
Total Time: 35 mins

Servings per Recipe: 8
Calories	253.0
Fat	9.3g
Cholesterol	20.9mg
Sodium	284.0mg
Carbohydrates	38.0g
Protein	4.6g

Ingredients

2 C. all-purpose flour
1 tbsp baking powder
1/4 tsp salt
1/4 C. brown sugar
1/3 C. butter, chilled and cut into 6
1/2 C. buttermilk

1 large apple, peeled and diced
1/3 C. granola cereal, broken up
brown sugar

Directions

1. Before you do anything, preheat the oven to 400 F.
2. Get a mixing bowl: Stir in it the flour, baking powder, salt, and sugar.
3. Mix in the butter until they become coarse. Add 1/2 C. buttermilk, apple, and granola.
4. Combine them well. Add the rest of the buttermilk gradually while mixing all the time.
5. Split the dough into two balls. Press them until they become 1 inch thick.
6. Slice each dough circle into 4 pieces. Lay them on a lined up baking sheet.
7. Cook them in the oven for 21 min.
8. Allow the scones to cool down completely. Serving with some icing of your choice.
9. Enjoy.

Country
Apple Crisp

Prep Time: 30 mins
Total Time: 1 hr

Servings per Recipe: 12
Calories   272.1
Fat   10.8g
Cholesterol   0.0mg
Sodium   78.0mg
Carbohydrates   42.2g
Protein   3.6g

Ingredients

Filling
10 C. sliced peeled apples
1/2 tsp cinnamon
1/4 tsp nutmeg
1/3 C. brown sugar
2 tbsps flour
Topping
2 C. granola cereal

2 tbsps flour
1/2 C. brown sugar
6 tbsps Hain safflower margarine, melted
1/4 tsp cinnamon

Directions

1. Before you do anything, preheat the oven to 350 F.
2. Get a mixing bowl: Stir in it the apples with cinnamon, nutmeg, brown sugar and flour.
3. Transfer the mixture to a greased baking dish.
4. Get a mixing bowl: Mix in it the margarine, brown sugar and flour.
5. Mix in it the granola with cinnamon. Sprinkle the mixture over the apple mix layer.
6. Cook it in the oven for 30 to 32 min. Serve it warm with some ice cream or yogurt.
7. Enjoy.

CHEDDAR
Chicken Empanadas

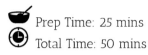

Prep Time: 25 mins
Total Time: 50 mins

Servings per Recipe: 15
Calories   155.4
Fat   9.5g
Cholesterol   30.5mg
Sodium   85.0mg
Carbohydrates   11.4g
Protein   6.1g

Ingredients

1 1/2 C. diced cooked chicken
2 granny smith apples, peeled and chopped
1 tsp. thyme
1 tbsp. honey
1 tbsp. butter
1/2 small white onion
1 garlic clove, minced
1/2 C. shredded cheddar cheese

salt and pepper
1 sheet puff pastry
1 egg, beaten

Directions

1. Set your oven to 400 degrees F before doing anything else and grease a baking sheet.
2. In a skillet, add the butter and cook until melted completely.
3. Add the apple, onion and garlic and stir fry until tender.
4. Stir in the chicken, honey, thyme, salt and pepper and remove from the heat.
5. Keep aside to cool slightly.
6. Add the cheddar cheese and stir to combine.
7. Place the puff pastry onto a lightly floured surface and roll into 1/8-inch thickness.
8. With a glass, cut the circles from the pastry.
9. Place about 1 tbsp. of the filling onto each circle.
10. Fold the dough over the filling and press the edges to seal.
11. In the bottom of the prepared baking sheet, arrange the empanadas and coat each with the egg wash.
12. Cook in the oven for about 25 minutes.
13. Enjoy warm.

Forest
Frost Empanadas

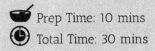 Prep Time: 10 mins

Total Time: 30 mins

Servings per Recipe: 12
Calories	238.7
Fat	13.1g
Cholesterol	2.5mg
Sodium	224.2mg
Carbohydrates	28.5g
Protein	2.4g

Ingredients

1 lb. fresh blackberries
1 C. fresh apple, pared and finely chopped
1/4 C. chopped walnuts
1/4 C. sugar
2 tbsp. flour
1 tsp. ground cinnamon
1 tsp. vanilla
1 dash salt

3 (9 inch) pie crusts
1 tbsp. butter
Garnish
1/2 tsp. cinnamon
2 tbsp. sugar

Directions

1. Set your oven to 400 degrees F before doing anything else and grease a baking sheet.
2. In a bowl, add the walnuts, apple, and flour, sugar, cinnamon, salt and vanilla and mix until well combined.
3. Gently fold in the blackberries.
4. Place the pastry onto a lightly floured surface and unroll it.
5. Then, cut into 12 (4 1/2-inch) circles.
6. Place about 2 tbsp. of the filling onto half of each circle, leaving about 1/2-inch border.
7. Fold the dough over the filling and press the edges to seal.
8. In a bowl, add 2 tbsp. of the sugar and 1/2 tsp. of the cinnamon and mix well.
9. In the bottom of the prepared baking sheet, arrange the empanadas.
10. Coat each empanada with the melted butter and then, dust with the cinnamon sugar.
11. Cook in the oven for about 18-20 minutes.
12. Enjoy warm.

ELIZABETH'S
Empanadas

Prep Time: 25 mins
Total Time: 3 hrs 45 mins

Servings per Recipe: 1
Calories	597.8
Fat	36.0g
Cholesterol	139.1mg
Sodium	227.3mg
Carbohydrates	61.9g
Protein	8.7g

Ingredients

1 large egg, beaten
2-3 tbsp. unsalted butter
3 large apples, cored, peeled, diced
1 dash turbinado sugar
3 tbsp. brown sugar
1 tsp. ground cinnamon
1 pinch salt
bench flour, for dusting
almond pastry
1 (17 1/3 oz.) boxes frozen puff pastry, thawed

Almond Pastry Crème
1 1/2 C. whole milk
1/2 C. sugar
2 tbsp. almond paste
1 pinch salt
4 large egg yolks
2 tbsp. cornstarch
3 tbsp. unsalted butter

Directions

1. For the almond pastry cream: in a heavy-bottomed pot, add the milk, almond paste, sugar and salt over medium heat and beat until well combined.
2. Cook until just boiling, mixing continuously.
3. In a bowl, add the egg yolks and cornstarch. And beat until thick and creamy.
4. Remove the milk mixture from the heat.
5. Slowly, add 1/4 C. of the milk mixture into the egg mixture, beating continuously until well combined.
6. Add the egg mixture into the pot of the remaining milk mixture and stir to combine.
7. Place the pan over the heat and cook for about 3 minutes, beating continuously.
8. Remove from the heat and stir in the butter until well combined.
9. Through a sieve, strain the pastry cream into a bowl.
10. Arrange a plastic wrap directly onto the surface of pastry cream and place in the fridge for about 3 hours.

11. In a skillet, add the butter over medium heat and cook until melted completely.
12. Add the apples and stir fry for about 5 minutes.
13. Add the brown sugar, salt and cinnamon and cook for about 10 minutes, mixing often.
14. Remove from the heat and with a fork, mash the mixture until a chunky applesauce like mixture forms.
15. Keep aside to cool completely.
16. Set your oven to 400 degrees F and line a baking sheet with the parchment paper.
17. After cooling of the apple mixture, gently fold in 1/4 C. of the pastry cream.
18. Place the puff pastry sheets onto a floured surface and separate them.
19. With a 4 1/2-inch round biscuit cutter, cut 4 large circles from each pastry sheet.
20. Place about 2 heaping tbsp. of the apple mixture onto the bottom half of each dough circle.
21. Coat the edges of each pastry circle with the egg wash.
22. Fold the dough over the filling and press the edges to seal.
23. In the bottom of the prepared baking sheet, arrange the empanadas.
24. With a knife, make 2 slits on top of each empanada.
25. Coat each empanada with the remaining egg wash and dust with the turbinado sugar.
26. Cook in the oven for about 20 minutes.
27. Remove from the oven and enjoy with the topping of the remaining almond pastry cream.

HARVEST
Crepes

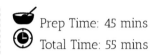

Prep Time: 45 mins
Total Time: 55 mins

Servings per Recipe: 8
Calories	215.7
Fat	13.0g
Cholesterol	82.0mg
Sodium	221.5mg
Carbohydrates	17.6g
Protein	7.6g

Ingredients

2 large eggs
1 C. milk
1/3 C. water
1 C. all-purpose flour, preferably bleached
1/4 tsp. salt
2 tbsp. butter, melted

butter, for coating the pan
3/4 C. Brie cheese, thinly sliced
2 small apples, thinly sliced
1 tbsp. butter, melted
1/4 C. walnuts, chopped

Directions

1. In a food processor, add the flour, 2 tbsp. of the melted butter, water, milk, eggs and salt and pulse until well combined.
2. Transfer the mixture into a bowl and place in the fridge for about 2 hours.
3. Grease a frying pan with a little butter and place over medium-high heat until heated through.
4. Place about 2-3 tbsp. of the mixture and tilt the pan to spread in a thin layer.
5. Cook for about 1 1/2 minutes, flipping once after 1 minute.
6. Repeat with the remaining mixture.
7. Set your oven to 375 degrees F.
8. Place 1 cheese slices over each crepe, followed by 3 apple slices.
9. Carefully, fold each crepe.
10. In the bottom of a 12x18-inch baking dish, arrange the crepes.
11. Coat the crepes with the remaining melted butter and top with the walnuts.
12. Cook in the oven for about 8-10 minutes.
13. Enjoy hot.

Big Apple Soufflé

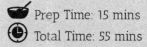 Prep Time: 15 mins
Total Time: 55 mins

Servings per Recipe: 8
Calories   254.0
Fat   3.4g
Cholesterol   1.2mg
Sodium   304.3mg
Carbohydrates   46.8g
Protein   10.6g

Ingredients

1 C. all-purpose flour
2 tbsp all-purpose flour
3 tbsp sugar
1/2 tsp salt
1/2 tsp cinnamon
2 C. fat free egg substitute
2 C. skim milk
1 tsp vanilla extract

2 tbsp unsalted margarine
6 apples, peeled and sliced thin
3 tbsp light brown sugar, firmly packed

Directions

1. Set your oven to 425 degrees F before doing anything else.
2. In a large bowl, mix together the flour, sugar, cinnamon and salt.
3. Make a well in the center of flour mixture.
4. Add the milk, egg substitute and vanilla in the well and beat until well combined.
5. In a 13x9-inch baking dish, add the margarine.
6. Place the baking dish in the oven for about 3 minutes.
7. Add the apples and gently, stir to coat.
8. Cook in the oven for about 5 minutes.
9. Place the egg mixture over the apples evenly and sprinkle with the brown sugar.
10. Cook in the oven for about 5 minutes.
11. Remove from the oven and serve immediately.

EASY
English Sorbet

Prep Time: 10 mins
Total Time: 10 mins

Servings per Recipe: 4
Calories	175 kcal
Fat	0.3 g
Carbohydrates	45.9 g
Protein	0.9 g
Cholesterol	0 mg
Sodium	4 mg

Ingredients

1 fresh pineapple - peeled, cored and
cut into chunks
2 large green apples, washed and sliced
1 1/4 tsps chopped fresh ginger

1 C. brewed green tea, chilled
1 C. mango sorbet or crushed ice

Directions

1. Add your ginger, apples, and pineapples into a juicer.
2. Add the tea to the juice then stir everything completely then add in the sorbet and stir the again until it is evenly combined.
3. Enjoy.

Hibachi
Backyard Beef

Prep Time: 5 mins
Total Time: 30 mins

Servings per Recipe: 2
Calories	558.8
Fat	39.9 g
Cholesterol	77.1 mg
Sodium	1574.0 mg
Carbohydrates	20.0 g
Protein	24.7 g

Ingredients

1/2 lb. beef rib eye roast, slices
3 tbsp soy sauce
3 tbsp sake
1 1/2 tbsp sesame oil
1 1/2 tbsp sugar
1/2 apple, grated to release juice

2 tbsp roasted and ground sesame seeds
2 garlic cloves, minced
1/4 tsp dry mustard

Directions

1. Place a skillet over medium heat and cook until heated through.
2. Add the sesame seeds and stir fry until toasted slightly.
3. Remove from the heat.
4. In a coffee grinder, add the sesame seeds and grind slightly.
5. In a bowl, add the sesame seeds and remaining ingredients except the beef slices and mix until well combined.
6. Add the beef slices and coat with the marinade generously.
7. Place in the fridge for about 7-8 hours.
8. Set your grill for medium heat and grease the grill grate.
9. Cook them onto the grill for about 2-3 minutes, flipping once half way through.
10. Enjoy hot.

TANGY
Cranberry Salad for March

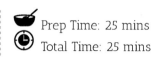

Prep Time: 25 mins
Total Time: 25 mins

Servings per Recipe: 12
Calories	276.2
Fat	20.5g
Cholesterol	8.7mg
Sodium	197.8mg
Carbohydrates	20.5g
Protein	5.2g

Ingredients

1/2 C. white sugar
1/2 C. lemon juice
2 tsp diced onions
1 tsp Dijon mustard
1/2 tsp salt
2/3 C. vegetable oil
1 tbsp poppy seed
1 head romaine lettuce, rinsed, dried
and torn into bite

4 oz. shredded Swiss cheese
1 C. cashews
1/4 C. dried cranberries
1 apple, peeled, cored and cubed
1 pear, cubed

Directions

1. In a food processor, add the onion, mustard, sugar, salt and lemon juice and pulse until combined finely.
2. While motor is running, slowly add the oil and pulse until smooth.
3. Add the poppy seeds and pulse for about 2-3 seconds.
4. In a bowl, add the romaine lettuce, pear, apple, cashews, cranberries and cheese and mix.
5. Place the dressing and toss to coat well.
6. Enjoy.

Vanilla
Pudding Bowls

🥣 Prep Time: 35 mins
🕐 Total Time: 35 mins

Servings per Recipe: 10
Calories	118.8
Fat	2.3g
Cholesterol	0.0mg
Sodium	2.5mg
Carbohydrates	26.4g
Protein	1.3g

Ingredients

2 medium bananas, diced
2 medium apples, diced
1 lemon, juice
1 (20 oz.) cans pineapple tidbits, drained, juice reserved
2 C. sliced strawberries

2 C. grapes
1/4 C. pecans, chopped
1 (1 1/2 oz.) box sugar-free instant vanilla pudding mix
1/2 C. water

Directions

1. In a bowl, add the apples, bananas and lemon juice and toss to coat well.
2. Add the grapes, strawberries, pineapple and pecans and gently, toss to coat.
3. In another bowl, add the pudding mix, pineapple juice and water and with a wire whisk, beat until smooth.
4. Add the pudding mixture into the bowl of the fruit and gently stir to combine.
5. Place in the fridge until using.
6. Enjoy chilled.

FRUIT SALAD
Casablanca

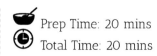

Prep Time: 20 mins
Total Time: 20 mins

Servings per Recipe: 5
Calories	127.8
Fat	1.5g
Cholesterol	4.4mg
Sodium	17.2mg
Carbohydrates	28.7g
Protein	2.5g

Ingredients

6 - 8 oz. vanilla yogurt
1 pint fresh strawberries, hulled and sliced
2 apples, peeled, cored and chopped
1 - 2 banana, peeled and sliced
1 orange, peeled and sectioned

1 tbsp sugar
1 orange, juiced

Directions

1. In a bowl, add all the ingredients and toss to coat well.
2. Enjoy.

Morning Mist Fruit Salad with Nuts

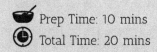 Prep Time: 10 mins

Total Time: 20 mins

Servings per Recipe: 4
Calories	1180.7
Fat	18.3g
Cholesterol	2.3mg
Sodium	130.5mg
Carbohydrates	268.5g
Protein	15.1g

Ingredients

Nuts
1 tsp peanut oil
1 tsp honey
2 tbsp white sugar
1/2 tsp vanilla
1/8 tsp salt
3/4 C. walnuts, chopped

Salad
2 green apples, cored, sliced
2 small red apples, cored, sliced
40 red seedless grapes
3/4 C. low-fat vanilla yogurt
2 tbsp lemon juice

Directions

1. For candied nuts: in a skillet, add the honey, peanut oil, vanilla, sugar and salt over medium heat and cook just boiling, mixing continuously.
2. Stir in the walnuts and cook until caramelized, mixing continuously.
3. Remove from the heat and stir the walnuts continuously for at least 1 minute.
4. Transfer the walnuts onto a plate and gently, toss to avoid the sticking.
5. Keep aside to cool completely.
6. Meanwhile, in a bowl, dip the apple slices into the lemon juice.
7. In a bowl, add all fruits, yogurt and candied walnuts and gently, stir to combine.
8. Enjoy.

SUNFLOWER
Sesame Fruit Salad

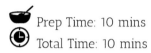 Prep Time: 10 mins
Total Time: 10 mins

Servings per Recipe: 1	
Calories	516.9
Fat	34.7g
Cholesterol	0.0mg
Sodium	611.0mg
Carbohydrates	52.9g
Protein	5.5g

Ingredients

2 tbsp olive oil
1 tbsp apple cider vinegar
1 tbsp honey
1/4 tsp salt
3/4 C. fresh spinach, torn
1/3 C. chopped apple
1/4 C. broccoli floret
2 tbsp raisins

2 dried apricots, chopped
1 tbsp sunflower seeds
2 tsp sesame seeds, toasted
1 tsp lemon juice

Directions

1. In a bowl, add the honey, vinegar, oil and salt and beat until well combined.
2. In another bowl, add the remaining ingredients and mix.
3. Pour the dressing over salad and toss to combine.

Fruit Salad
in Farsi

🍲 Prep Time: 5 mins
🕐 Total Time: 5 mins

Servings per Recipe: 6

Calories	442.5
Fat	12.7g
Cholesterol	0.0mg
Sodium	82.8mg
Carbohydrates	84.2g
Protein	8.1g

Ingredients

2 seedless oranges, peeled and cored
2 apples, peeled and cored
2 bananas, sliced
2 C. pitted dates, chopped
1 C. dried figs, chopped

1 C. orange juice
1 C. almonds, chopped

Directions

1. In a bowl, add fruit and orange juice and gently, stir to combine.
2. Place the almonds on top.
3. Cover the bowl and place in the fridge or about 4-5 hours.
4. Enjoy chilled.

SONOMA
Fruit Salad

Prep Time: 20 mins
Total Time: 20 mins

Servings per Recipe: 4
Calories	468.8
Fat	26.3g
Cholesterol	0.0mg
Sodium	214.5mg
Carbohydrates	62.3g
Protein	4.2g

Ingredients

Salad
1 green apple, cored and chopped
1 ripe avocado, peeled, pitted and chopped
1 banana, peeled and chopped
1 (11 oz.) cans mandarin oranges, drained
1/4 C. raisins
1/4 C. nuts, chopped

Dressing
1 tsp lemon juice
1/4 C. orange juice
1/4 C. canola oil
1/3 C. honey
1/4 tsp Dijon mustard
1/4 tsp salt
1 1/2 tsp poppy seeds

Directions

1. For the salad: in a bowl, add all the ingredients and mix well.
2. For the dressing: in another bowl, add all the ingredients and beat until well combined.
3. Place the dressing over salad and gently, stir to combine.
4. Enjoy.

Fruit Salad
Accra

Prep Time: 15 mins
Total Time: 15 mins

Servings per Recipe: 10
Calories	136.5
Fat	1.5g
Cholesterol	0.0mg
Sodium	13.0mg
Carbohydrates	32.3g
Protein	1.5g

Ingredients

4 ripe papayas, peeled, seeded and chopped
2 red apples, cored and chopped
2 ripe bananas, peeled and sliced
1 (16 oz.) cans pineapple tidbits, well-drained

1 C. fresh orange juice
1 tbsp granulated sugar
1/2 tsp ground cinnamon
1/3 C. sweetened flaked coconut

Directions

1. In a bowl, add all the ingredients except the coconut and toss to coat well.
2. Cover the bowl and place in the fridge to chill completely.
3. Enjoy with a topping of the coconut.

AFRICAN
Orange Bowls

Prep Time: 20 mins
Total Time: 20 mins

Servings per Recipe: 4
Calories   218.2
Fat   0.6g
Cholesterol   0.0mg
Sodium   2.0mg
Carbohydrates   55.0g
Protein   2.7g

Ingredients

1/4 melon, cubed
2 apples, cubed
2 bananas, sliced
5 oranges, peeled, seeded and chopped
3/4 C. orange juice
1/4 C. lemon juice

2 tbsp sugar
1 tsp vanilla
1/2 tsp cinnamon

Directions

1. In a bowl, add all the ingredients and gently, toss to coat well.
2. Place in the fridge to chill completely.
3. Enjoy chilled.

Fruit Salad
Arabia

🥣 Prep Time: 10 mins
🕐 Total Time: 15 mins

Servings per Recipe: 6
Calories	200.7
Fat	0.3g
Cholesterol	0.0mg
Sodium	17.8mg
Carbohydrates	52.8g
Protein	1.8g

Ingredients

1 medium cantaloupe, peeled and cubed
2 medium seedless oranges, peeled
sectioned and sections halved
2 medium apples, peeled cored and cubed
1/2 C. seedless raisin
Sauce

1/2 C. honey
2 tbsp water
1/2 tsp ground cardamom
1/4 C. fresh lemon juice

Directions

1. For the sauce: in a pot, add the cardamom, honey and water and cook until boiling, mixing occasionally.
2. Cook for about 2 minutes, mixing occasionally.
3. Remove from the heat and stir in the lemon juice.
4. Keep aside to cool completely.
5. In a bowl, add the fruit and cooled sauce and toss to coat well.
6. Place in the fridge to chill.
7. Enjoy chilled.

LATE OCTOBER
Lunch Box

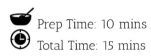 Prep Time: 10 mins

Total Time: 15 mins

Servings per Recipe: 12

Calories	70.1
Fat	0.9g
Cholesterol	0.4mg
Sodium	20.6mg
Carbohydrates	15.6g
Protein	1.1g

Ingredients

2 medium granny smith apples, cored and cut into wedges
1 C. halved red seedless grapes
1 (11 oz.) cans mandarin orange segments, drained
1 1/2 C. miniature marshmallows,

optional
1 (8 oz.) containers low-fat vanilla yogurt
2 tbsp chopped nuts
1 lime, zest

Directions

1. In a bowl, add all the ingredients except walnuts and gently stir to combine.
2. Top with the nuts walnuts evenly.
3. Cover the bowl and place in the fridge to chill completely.
4. Enjoy chilled.

Whipped Apple and Banana Salad

🥣 Prep Time: 5 mins
🕐 Total Time: 5 mins

Servings per Recipe: 1
Calories	1905.7
Fat	5.4g
Cholesterol	2.7mg
Sodium	57.2mg
Carbohydrates	497.4g
Protein	19.8g

Ingredients

1 banana, chopped to size of grapes
20 seedless grapes
1/2 apple, chopped to size of grapes
1 tbsp sugar-free strawberry jelly

1 tbsp fat-free whipped topping
1 fresh cherries

Directions

1. In a bowl, add all ingredients except whipped topping and cherry and gently, stir to combine.
2. Place the whipped topping on top and enjoy with a garnishing of the cherry.

HAPPY
Fruit Salad

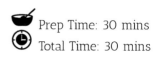

Prep Time: 30 mins
Total Time: 30 mins

Servings per Recipe: 4
Calories	197.2
Fat	6.5g
Cholesterol	12.6mg
Sodium	18.9mg
Carbohydrates	35.6g
Protein	2.5g

Ingredients

1/2 C. sour cream
1/4 C. frozen orange juice concentrate, thawed
2 tsp honey
1 C. strawberry, halves
1 C. red apple, slices

1 C. green seedless grape
1 (11 oz.) cans mandarin orange segments, well drained
mixed salad green

Directions

1. In a bowl, add the honey, sour cream and orange juice and beat until well combined.
2. In the bottom of a bowl, arrange the salad greens and top with the salad.
3. Enjoy with a topping of the dressing.

Fruit Salad
Tampa

Prep Time: 15 mins
Total Time: 15 mins

Servings per Recipe: 10
Calories	178.2
Fat	0.5g
Cholesterol	0.0mg
Sodium	166.1mg
Carbohydrates	45.6g
Protein	1.4g

Ingredients

3 apples, chopped
1 (11 oz.) cans mandarin oranges, drained
2 (15 oz.) cans pineapple tidbits, drained
save juice
3 bananas, chopped
1 pint strawberry, sliced

3 tbsp Tang orange crystals
1 (4 oz.) boxes instant vanilla pudding

Directions

1. In a bowl, add the pineapple juice and pudding and mix until well combined.
2. Add the Tang and stir to combine.
3. Add the fruit and gently, stir to combine.
4. Refrigerate to chill completely.
5. Enjoy chilled.

PINEAPPLE
Papaya Salad

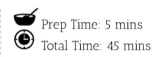 Prep Time: 5 mins

Total Time: 45 mins

Servings per Recipe: 6

Calories	86.1
Fat	0.3g
Cholesterol	0.0mg
Sodium	1.8mg
Carbohydrates	22.3g
Protein	0.9g

Ingredients

1/3 papaya, chopped
1/3 pineapple, chunked
2 bananas, sliced
2 cored tart apples, chopped

1 lime, juice
1 ripe orange, juice

Directions

1. In a bowl, add all the ingredients and gently, toss to coat well.
2. Keep aside for about 45 minutes.
3. Enjoy.

Latin
Banana Lunch Box Salad

🍲 Prep Time: 10 mins
🕐 Total Time: 20 mins

Servings per Recipe: 6
Calories   140.7
Fat   0.4g
Cholesterol   0.0mg
Sodium   30.3mg
Carbohydrates   34.2g
Protein   3.0g

Ingredients

2 firm bananas, peeled and sliced
2 apples, cored and chopped
1 (15 oz.) cans mandarin oranges, drained
1 tbsp honey
1/2-1 tsp cinnamon
1/2 C. pineapple juice

2 - 3 tbsp lemon juice
3 egg whites
1 1/2 tbsp sugar

Directions

1. Set your oven to 450 degrees F before doing anything else.
2. In a casserole dish, place all the fruit, honey, pineapple juice, lemon juice and cinnamon and mix until well combined.
3. Ina glass bowl, add the egg whites and beat until frothy.
4. Slowly add the sugar, beating continuously until stiff peaks form.
5. Place the meringue over the fruit mixture evenly.
6. Cook in the oven for about 5-10 minutes.
7. Enjoy warm.

GERMAN
Plum Salad

Prep Time: 10 mins
Total Time: 10 mins

Servings per Recipe: 4
Calories   415.3
Fat   8.1g
Cholesterol   0.0mg
Sodium   10.8mg
Carbohydrates   85.5g
Protein   6.5g

Ingredients

2 red plums, pitted and chopped
4 bananas, chopped
4 apples, cored and chopped
1 lemon, juice

4 tbsp sugar
1 C. granola cereal

Directions

1. In a bowl, add the sugar and lemon juice and beat until sugar is dissolved.
2. In another bowl, add the fruit and mix well.
3. add the sugar mixture and granola and mix until well combined.
4. Enjoy.

Fruit Salad
Autumns

🥣 Prep Time: 15 mins
🕐 Total Time: 17 mins

Servings per Recipe: 12

Calories	82.8
Fat	3.3g
Cholesterol	0.0mg
Sodium	4.7mg
Carbohydrates	13.6g
Protein	1.3g

Ingredients

1 (1/4 oz.) package unflavored gelatin
1 C. cranberry-grape juice, chilled
1 C. cranberry-grape juice, boiling
2 C. fresh cranberries, chopped in a food processor
1 (15 oz.) cans pineapple tidbits, drained

1 C. red seedless grapes, halved
1 apple, cored and chopped
3/4 C. mini marshmallows, optional
1/2 C. toasted pecans, chopped

Directions

1. In a bowl, add 1 C. of the chilled juice and sprinkle with the gelatin.
2. Keep aside for about 1 minute.
3. Now, add the boiling juice and stir until the gelatin dissolves completely.
4. Place in the fridge to just chill.
5. Remove from the fridge and stir in the pineapple, cranberries, apple, grapes, pecans and marshmallows until well combined.
6. Place in the fridge for about 4 hours.
7. Enjoy chilled.

FIVE-SPICE
Mango Salad

Prep Time: 10 mins
Total Time: 2 hrs 10 mins

Servings per Recipe: 4

Calories	87.5
Fat	0.3g
Cholesterol	0.0mg
Sodium	1.9mg
Carbohydrates	22.5g
Protein	0.8g

Ingredients

1 medium ripe mango, sliced
1 medium ripe banana, sliced
3/4-1 C. halved strawberry
1 medium apple, chopped
3 tbsp Splenda sugar substitute

1/4 tsp Chinese five spice powder
1/4 tsp vanilla extract
1 tsp lemon juice

Directions

1. In a bowl, add all the ingredients and mix well.
2. Cover the bowl and refrigerate for about 2-4 hours.
3. Enjoy chilled.

Jamaican
Apple Fruit Salad

🥣 Prep Time: 30 mins
🕐 Total Time: 30 mins

Servings per Recipe: 5
Calories	272.3
Fat	13.4g
Cholesterol	12.4mg
Sodium	91.0mg
Carbohydrates	39.2g
Protein	2.8g

Ingredients

2 large sweet apples, chunked
2 oranges, peeled and chunked
1/2 C. pineapple chunks
1 banana, sliced
1/2 C. sweetened flaked coconut, toasted
1/2 C. sweetened flaked coconut

1/4 C. coconut milk
2 oz. cream cheese, softened
2 tsp sugar

Directions

1. Set your oven to 300 degrees F before doing anything else.
2. Place the coconut onto an ungreased baking sheet in an even layer.
3. Cook in the oven for about 3-5 minutes.
4. remove from the oven and keep aside to cool.
5. In a bowl, add the pineapple, apples, banana, oranges, toasted coconut, and coconut milk and mix well.
6. In another bowl, add the cream cheese and sugar and beat until creamy and smooth.
7. Place the cream cheese mixture in the bowl of the fruit mixture and gently, stir to combine.
8. Enjoy.

ENJOY THE RECIPES?
KEEP ON COOKING
WITH 6 MORE FREE COOKBOOKS!

Visit our website and simply enter your email address to join the club and receive your 6 cookbooks.

http://booksumo.com/magnet

https://www.instagram.com/booksumopress/

https://www.facebook.com/booksumo/

.

Printed in Great Britain
by Amazon